BASEMENT PRIEST

REFLECTIONS 1970-2020

John Boos M.Afr

Basement Priest
Copyright © 2021 by John Boos M.Afr

All rights reserved. No part of this publication may be reproduced, distributed, or transmitted in any form or by any means, including photocopying, recording, or other electronic or mechanical methods, without the prior written permission of the author, except in the case of brief quotations embodied in critical reviews and certain other non-commercial uses permitted by copyright law.

Tellwell Talent
www.tellwell.ca

ISBN
978-0-2288-4237-8 (Hardcover)
978-0-2288-4236-1 (Paperback)
978-0-2288-4238-5 (eBook)

FOREWORD

Truth should be ever-present in the heart and mind of those who seek. Yet, it can be resisted, twisted, and misdirected. Truth, however, can never be changed, it remains. It is the essential communication, of highest value.

BASEMENT PRIEST by Fr John Boos is a 'cannot-put-down' book of this most important value. The 'pearl of great price', Jesus-Christ, is Truth itself, and is the key to his work. How Truth has interacted with culture in history, philosophy, ideology, and the struggle against its demise are highlighted in these pages.

Fr. John illuminates the Four Necessities of the Divine Plan as they unfold in history, as salvation contacts human experience. This is the very dynamic of *BASEMENT PRIEST*. He leads us through the interaction of the "WORD", the great "I AM", the Covenants, the Incarnation, and reveals the effects it creates, both negative and positive. We see great heresies defined, and replied to by Church's Councils. The revelation of humility, its mystery in Christ, the Trinity, the Eucharist, Transubstantiation, and the Mass itself is abundantly clarified. *BASEMENT PRIEST* presents an apologetic of insight and exegesis which empowers and lifts both faith and reason. The reader is invited to observe the "Word" as it communicates with human experience. The meaning of Jesus "lifted up" on the Cross, the detailed examination of his burial and resurrection, with compelling reason challenges us to faith and resolution with deeper understanding. This too flows into the evidence shown by the Shroud of Turin.

Faith and Reason ought never to be separate; Reason informed by Faith illuminates the "Word", Christ himself. With this, the author reveals the fallacies of the 'secret knowledge' of Gnosticism and the Reformation. Luther's teachings for example, of 'faith alone' and 'Scripture alone' gave birth to the great sin of *"presumption"* which grew out of a Church soiled by simony and corruption. This thesis is shown in the rise of Protestantism and the demise of Truth which resulted. The staggering effects of Luther's reductionism formed the basis of the modern alienation from both God and Reason and influenced the demise of culture itself, including the present moment.

Two World Wars and the terrible loss of life, have all had consequences on Faith and Reason. The stark tragedy of the 1968 Winnipeg Statement and its concurrent temptation to accept a contraceptive mentality invaded the Church, and was resisted by the necessity of Truth in matrimonial love, taught so aptly by the Humanae Vitae of Paul VI.

To these clashes, Fr John illustrates the backdrop of the "Word", actively working. The profound truths of the Church founded on Peter, the Eucharist, and Paul's preaching, all built the visible Church, not the invisible one of Luther and the Reformers, which is a clear and persistent sign of the promise of Christ, **"I am with you always, even to the end of the age"**. This stunning reality of God made flesh and blood and its consequences, which is in fact our Eucharistic Lord, confounds all heresies. His incarnation into our human experience is continuous. This revelation is the very 'source and summit' of our Faith. Importantly, *BASEMENT PRIEST* also testifies to the Virgin Mary and her femininity which displaces the exclusively male claim to spirituality. She initiates changes to deepen our understanding of feminine attributes, as revealed by God's communication and will.

The book is also and perhaps most importantly a recognition of the great need for a fundamental education of Catholic laity in matters of Faith and Reason. It shows an urgency to correct the absence of basic knowledge of History and Faith so prevalent today among Catholic-Christians, which maintains the current demise of truth in culture. Fr. John sees the need to evangelize, and responds with a work of catechesis and apologetics, a prototype for the necessary religious education. It should also interest all denominations of those professing to be Christians.

BASEMENT PRIEST offers the reader the means of navigating the past, understanding the present, and by so doing serving the future. It belongs on the desk of every Christian educator, parent, clerical member, and individual seeking a deeper understanding of this present moment in history.

Paul Coates B.A. B.ED. M.DIV

PREFACE

The last few years in my basement flat, apart from leaving it to help out in the Parishes of Scarborough in Toronto and those of Durham of Ontario Province, have helped me to reflect on many issues, most of them concerning Faith, its acceptance or rejection by today's secular culture, and how its very common misrepresentations could be corrected and clarified. I had to begin by understanding myself.

Born in Trinidad, West Indies, in 1937, to a working-class family, I have lived through what may have been perhaps the most fantastic and important 80 years of all human history. World War l (1914-1918) saw my family involved, and the Spanish Civil War (1936-1939) welcomed me into the world. This was followed by World War ll (1939-1945), the Cold War (1945-1989), the Korean War (1950-1953), the Vietnamese War (1956-1975), the Second Vatican Council (1962-1965), the Moon landings (1969 et seq), the Encyclical **Humanae Vitae** (1968), the Sexual Revolution (1965–1977) – years during which hundreds of millions were killed and/or displaced, new nations were born, border-lines were re-drawn, political philosophies directed how nations were to live – and I am still alive, even in these ongoing nuclear and electronic ages! The past 80 years have seen the rise and fall of big and small dictators – Stalin, Hitler, Mussolini, Mao, Pol Pot, Ho Shi Minh, Castro, Idi Amin, Mugabe, and the super-important papacies of Pius Xll,

John XXIII, Paul VI, John-Paul II, and Benedict XVI. Everything being considered, a most interesting time. But….

This 21st century didn't happen by itself; it has been formed by the preceding centuries, their histories, philosophies, wars, their immense cultural changes. How will it affect the succeeding ones?

My Primary and Secondary Educations were followed by Legal studies, resulting in my Admission to the Bar in 1975, which was upgraded in 1987. I left the profession of Law for various reasons, joined the Society of Missionaries of Africa in 1963, and was ordained to the Catholic priesthood in 1970. There followed 50 most interesting years as a missionary in Africa and other countries, and at the present moment my Superiors have allowed me to remain in semi-retirement to aid the Archdiocese of Toronto.

The issues of these reflections concern mainly Faith and religion as understood by my Church, and thus this book is both catechetic and apologetic, no holds barred. The use of the Bible is necessary and recommended. Due to the proximity of some of the themes, there's a bit of necessary repetition here and there, but all are my way of trying to find the "big picture", to "smell the roses", as it were.

I trust the reader will enjoy them as much as I did in putting them together.

Fr John Boos MAfr

TABLE OF CONTENTS

Foreword iii
Preface vii

Chapter 1   The Divine Plan 1
Chapter 2   Jesus the Christ 9
Chapter 3   The WORD 15
Chapter 4   The Covenants 23
Chapter 5   The Incarnation 29
Chapter 6   Humility 42
Chapter 7   Didacticism 51
Chapter 8   Transubstantiation 65
Chapter 9   The Mass 84
Chapter 10   Resurrection Proof 89
Chapter 11   The Trinity 99
Chapter 12   The Reformation 108
Chapter 13   The Bible Alone 135
Chapter 14   Faith Alone 145
Chapter 15   Peter and Paul 157
Chapter 16   the Rock 164
Chapter 17   Feminine Element 174
Chapter 18   Jesus' Presence 184
Chapter 19   Jesus Lifted Up 194
Chapter 20   The Catholic Family 200

CHAPTER 1

The Divine Plan

Four Necessities of Mystery

Anything which exists, or can exist – object, event, or person – may become a necessity. Without the presence and action of the person, thing or event, any expected result would either be an abject failure, or utterly impossible to attain. Thus, two hands are necessary for clapping, an operation may be necessary in the case of a severe illness, water is necessary for plants to grow and produce fruit, flowers, and so on. Such necessities are logical and evidential unto themselves.

However, when the question of the salvation of all mankind without exception is concerned, different concepts present themselves, those of religious and/or metaphysical necessities, understandable by their own rules, and by those who accept them. If as Catholic-Christians we believe and maintain that Our Lord Jesus-Christ came into our humanity and history so that all mankind, made in the image and likeness of Almighty God (**Gen.1:26-27**), then the method and intention of this salvation could only come, necessarily, from a Divine Plan, not of human making. This Plan would take place in the workings of human history, lived by all human beings, and would involve several stages or Necessities, each of which would include a Mystery, acceptable to all by Faith, which of itself is a gift from the Almighty.

The **Incarnation of Jesus**, made possible by the *"Fiat"* of Our Lady (**Lk.1:38**), was of itself not only possible or feasible, but was above all, a **First Necessity**. No human could possibly have imagined such a plan for mankind's salvation. It was a plan that God alone could have designed. Could any mere man assure the salvation of all humanity? Only a God who made himself "touchable", to whom one could relate and pray in human terms, could be lived with and loved.

First to Jesus himself. Did he really exist? Or was his story merely a fantasy cooked up by a few rebel Jewish fishermen?

In fact, his existence was never seriously denied by the first Christians or non-Christians. On the contrary, over a dozen non-Christian historians and commentators on the new "sect" of the first centuries attest to his existence, acts, and teaching, and often refer to the group he had founded. (See Chap.2 – Jesus Christ). But Jesus himself elicited serious questions on the part of certain believers, many of whom were, or would become, heretics, - those who offer an "opinion or doctrine contrary to the orthodox tenets of a religious body or church" (Collins English Dictionary). (See Chap. 5 – The Incarnation). Here now are two of the earliest and greatest of heresies.

The Arians (c.275 – 375AD) and Nestorians (c.420 AD to today) held that he was only fully human, although an extra-ordinary one. However, if he were only human, even though extraordinary, would he have been able to rescue *all* mankind from its guilt, sin, and evil propensities, as he claimed? He himself would be subject to sickness, weaknesses, sin, and guilt, common to every human. Besides, could only *one* such extraordinary human have been born through *all* the centuries and from *all* the generations of mankind? Such a proposition is itself ridiculous.

The Monophysites (550+ AD) claimed that he was really divine, having only a divine nature, his human form being merely a disguise. If this were so, he would have been clearly outside of our common human experience, his saving power would be merely a divine imposition, unacceptable to the common run of humanity, and possibly leading to superstitions.

To counter these, St Athanasius (296 - 373 AD) proposed that Jesus had in fact been endowed with dual natures, one human, one divine, from the very moment of conception in Mary's womb. That is, these dual natures of Jesus made of the Incarnation a necessity in itself, as both natures would be operative during all his life. His human nature, his compassion for others and its needs, joined itself to ours in everything but sin (**Heb.2:14-18**; **4:15**). His divine nature expressed itself in his teachings – the Our Father, the Beatitudes, the parables, the New Commandment (**Jn.13:34**), and the Golden Rule (**Lk.6:31**; **Mt.7:12**), his cures of the sick and raising of the dead, his many miracles. These two natures of Jesus were of themselves combined into the **First Necessity** we call **the Incarnation**, the God-man Jesus the Christ. Theology calls this the *hypostatic union*, the miracle of the union of two natures in one Person (**Council of Chalcedon, 451 AD**).

The **Condemnation of Jesus** by the Gentiles and Jews (**Mt.26:47-27:66**; **Mk.14:43-15:39**; **Lk.23:1-49**; **Jn.18:1-19:37**), his sufferings, crucifixion, and death, was the **Second Necessity**. It was necessary to show, even in this most excruciating and humiliating series of rejections, that the man Jesus was not exempt from the derision and injustices which so many of his fellow-humans experience. It can be affirmed that this most bestial and brutal of executions was also necessary, as an example to his and future generations. (**Jn.12:32** – *"And when I am lifted up from the earth, I shall draw all men to myself".* Cf. **Num.21:4-9**) – he knew that mankind would have to choose. Many would accept him, many would not, and Jesus was prepared to die for this truth. (See Chap. 19 – Jesus Lifted Up).

Jesus knew that his radically new interpretation of the Law of Moses [with its 613 basic precepts] would eventually bring him into conflict with the theocratic Jewish authorities. So, after having cured someone he often forbade the person to spread the good news around, i.e. so as not to draw attention to himself (**Mt.8:4; 9:31, 16:20; Mk. 5:43, 8:26; Lk.5:14**). But he was often not successful, as the cured person was only too glad to express his joy of recovery, to be received once more into normal Jewish society. Jesus knew the danger of these public exhibitions of joy, and his efforts to gain time to do his work were not all successful. He was betrayed to the Jewish authorities, as he had foretold, but he promised that after his death he would rise again after three days (**Mt.16:21; 17:23; 20:18-19**). The crucifixion and death of Jesus were therefore a combined Necessity also. Any other plan of action would have been commonplace, mere historical fact, or forgotten.

Having dual natures meant that it was the human Jesus and his human nature who had been killed, his divinity remained untouched. He had the power to lay down his life, and power to take it up again (**Jn.10:18**). His **Resurrection** is therefore the **Third Necessity**. A mere human could not conquer death, only one of dual natures could, and Jesus lives again because of the fullness of divinity in him. (**Col.2:9**).

All through his life, from the moment of conception to his journeys on the dusty pathways of Palestine, to his death on the Cross, to his Resurrection in the Holy Sepulchre, Jesus has shown the duality of his natures. It is only by recognising the necessities of his Incarnation, Death and Resurrection that one can fully accept the necessity of Jesus himself, God-man born into humanity. <u>It was necessary for him to be born, suffer, die and rise again, for humans to accede to salvation</u>.

The last and possibly the most important necessity – at least for Jesus himself, and for our way of thinking – was the thought: *What will happen to my message when I leave? What will become of it?* Important considerations, again, which only divine ingenuity can resolve.

Given the natural urge and tendency of peoples to profess their authentic identities by separating into clans, groups and nations, Jesus did that which only a God could have imagined – he left behind a **visible body of men who would continue the message, with the assurance that it would never be falsified, that evil would not prevail (**Mt. 16:13-20**). He even promised that the Holy Spirit would come (**Jn.15:26**) and would teach them all things to come after his departure, as they were still unable to understand everything (**Jn.16:12-13**). He even promised to be always with them, until the end of the age (**Mt.28:20**). On saying these things, <u>Jesus implied that there would be developments in the faith</u> through the coming centuries. This in fact did happen, and is still happening. Many groups have separated, and are still separating from the original body founded by Jesus. Many are still unable to accept the developments of the faith guaranteed by the presence of the Holy Spirit, following the promise of Our Lord; and at Pentecost the Spirit came, as had been promised (**Acts 2:1-13**).

Jesus' misgivings were realised only too well. In 2020 there are probably over 47,000 non-Catholic sects world-wide, many being only nominally Christian. [The 2018 findings of the U.S. Gordon-Conwell Evangelical seminary].

However, the exclusive term "Church" has been widened in the last 150 years by a majority of Protestant groups to mean the "church" of all who believe in Jesus, even vaguely. This vague amorphous form the Catholic Church obviously does not and cannot accept. Sensing the dire need for a central teaching authority for the multitude of dissenting "churches", a loss which took place in the 16th century, this modern Protestant appellation [from the "Branch Theory" of Wm. Palmer (1803-1885] seems to be merely a justification of an inability to find a central authority again, including a serious need for such authority. Obviously, a general return to "Rome" would be to admit that the whole exercise of the Reformation was wrong and sinful, going against the very will and intention of Jesus. So, onward with the idea of "churches"…

This appellation is doomed to fail, as <u>every believer in Jesus then becomes his own spiritual authority</u>, i.e. by free interpretation of the Bible, and by faith alone, such tenets having been proposed by the 16th century Reformation. (See <u>Chap. 13 – Sola Scriptura</u> and <u>Chap. 14 – Sola Fide</u>). The amorphous quality of vague belief in Jesus is also most probably the reason for the upsurge of the many "Mega-churches", "Community churches", or "Family churches", which have blossomed in recent years, as means of calling back to some form of "worship" the hundreds of millions who have no definite bond to an established "church", but who in some way have retained a vague belief in Jesus our Saviour, hoping that some sense of morality and sense of life could be given to their families. More such "churches" may be on the way.…..

The Catholic Church has been built, not to be influenced by the new trends and/or pressures occurring throughout the centuries, but for eternity. She has been commissioned to carry this message to "the nations" (**Mt.28: 18-20**), guaranteed by the Holy Spirit (**Jn.16:12-15**). This Church therefore teaches that **Jesus and herself are one combined Fourth Necessity**, as proclaimed by the encyclical the *"Mystical Body of Christ"*, of Pope Pius Xll:

(*Mystici Corporis Christi* – Pius Xll, 1943 – No. 22. *"Actually, only those are to be included as members of the Church, are those who have been baptised and profess the true faith, and who have not been so unfortunate as to separate themselves from the unity of the Body, or been excluded by legitimate authority for grave faults committed"*).

***Hypostatic Union** - The "**hypostatic union**" is an important **theological concept** concerning the person and work of Jesus Christ. It basically says that Jesus Christ is one Person, having two natures (divine and human). A normal human person is a hypostasis endowed with reason. Moreover, hypostasis and nature are related to each other in such a manner that the hypostasis is the bearer of the nature and the ultimate subject of all being and acting, while the nature is that through which the hypostasis exists and acts.

The Council of Chalcedon [451 AD] issued the Chalcedonian Definition, which repudiated the notion of a single nature in Christ, and declared that he has two natures in one Person and hypostasis. It also insisted on the completeness of his two natures: Godhead and manhood.

This **visible body, the "Catholic Church" of 2020, claims to be the same and only one founded by Jesus in approximately 33 AD. It continues to be united to the present Pope, the 265th chronological successor of Peter the Fisherman (**Mt.4:18; 16:13-20**; **Jn.21:15-17**). This body of men and women, called "Christians" in Antioch of Syria in the first century (**Acts 11:26**), was called for the first time ever the "Catholic Church" by St Ignatius of Antioch in

107AD in his letter "To the Smyrnaeans 8:2", while on his way to Rome to be martyred in the Colosseum.

> Thus says Israel's king
> And his redeemer, Yahweh Sabaoth:
> I am the first and the last,
> There is no other God besides me.
> Who is like me? Let him stand up and speak,
> Let him show himself and argue it out before me.
> Who from the beginning foretold the future?
> Let them tell us what is yet to come.
> Have no fear, do not be afraid;
> Have I not told you and revealed it long ago?
> You are my witnesses, is there any God besides me?
> There is no Rock; I know of none.
>
> (Is.44:6-8 – See <u>Chap. 16 – The Rock</u>)

-o-o-o-o-o-o-o-

CHAPTER **2**

Jesus the Christ

His Existence

For those who may doubt the very existence of Jesus, here is a list of the **ancient sources**, both secular and religious.

Biblical Sources:

The whole New Testament – 27 books - is irrefutable evidence of his existence.
- The life of the Church through 2000 years, with the good and bad (preceded by the 46 Old Testament books).
- Christ's own admission (*"I came to fulfill"* - **Mt.5:17; Rm.10:4**) - the Jewish Prophecies and Mosaic Law.

Extra-Biblical Sources: (All numbers refer to AD = Anno Domini, a "Year of the Lord")

Emperors Tiberius (14-37) or Claudius (41-54) – decree referring implicitly to the Resurrection on an inscription found in Nazareth.

Flavius Josephus (37-100) – non-Christian Jewish historian; refers to Christ, on information given possibly by Catholic-Christian scribes.

Tacitus (55-117)- Roman historian. Refers to Jesus.

Lucian (2nd C) – Greek satirist against the Church– but never denies the historicity of Jesus.

Suetonius (c.120) - refers to "Chrestus", whose followers were making disturbances in Rome, and were expelled for this.

Pliny the Younger (c.112) – Governor of Bithynia; refers to Catholic-Christians killed by him, as followers of Christ.

Thallus (c.52) – Samaritan-born historian; Refers to the darkening of the sun at the crucifixion as an "eclipse" of the sun.

Julius Africanus (c. 221) – refers to Thallus' theory as impossible, as Jesus died at the full moon Passover. (Both therefore implicitly refer to the historicity of Jesus himself).

Mara bar Serapion (c.73) – refers to Christ as a King. (Letter in the British Museum).

Jewish Talmud (final compilation in 500) – refers to the "hanging" of Yeshua (Jesus).

Shimeon ben 'Azzai – refers to Jesus in a scroll found in Jerusalem.

Celsus (2nd C.)- an enemy of Catholic-Christians; never questioned the historicity of Jesus.

Porphyry of Tyre (b. 233) – wrote 15 books against the Catholic-Christian faith; but never denied the historicity of Jesus.

The Patristic Fathers of the Church – Polycarp, Irenaeus etc.

<u>Catacombs of Rome</u> – 600 miles of underground galleries (4 million graves), with many Catholic-Christian symbols.

Modern Sources

Up to the mid-1550s, the Catholic Church – excluding dissident groups (mainly Waldensians and Nestorians), but including the Orthodox Church, (which had separated in 1054 AD) - was the main witness to the impossible-to-believe event which had taken place at the start of our epoch, that <u>Almighty God Himself had entered into human history</u> in the Person of His Son, Jesus the Christ, the very fulfilment of the ancient Jewish prophecies.

The story of Jesus the Christ (from *chrism*, meaning the 'anointed') is universally known, so it would not be necessary to detail it all now. Suffice it to say that through the 1550 years of kingdoms, empires, kings, emperors, revolutions, wars, the global pandemics and heresies of her history, the Catholic Church had managed to keep alive in the Civilisation built by herself in the West, the reality of the Person of Our Lord. Through her Councils, her theologians, her many saints, martyrs, and confessors, all of whom had included persons of both sexes, she had kept alive the living image of Jesus and His saving message. For the Church, Jesus the Person was not just a figment of the imagination, not just a myth, but a real Someone who gave sense to the life of the world, a reason to be alive, and a hope that the suffering of the world and its inhabitants would eventually come to an end with his Second Coming. At the promised Judgement, everyone's acts would be brought to light.

For the Church of the 21st century, this is still the case. She still continues to teach as commanded by Our Lord, still sends out her missionaries, still has her Pope, her Councils, her great thinkers, her martyrs, her Sacraments, and for her, Jesus is the living proof of the love of the Almighty for the world's many peoples. In doing so, she is the infallible Source of Truth guaranteed by the gift of the Spirit, promised by Jesus in **Jn.16:4-15.** She is his witness to the Truth.

All this changed in the 16th century. Divorcing themselves from the Church, her teaching, rites, liturgy, hierarchy, and authority, seven "Reformers" – Luther, Melanchthon, Calvin, Knox, Bucer, Zwingli, and the English king, Henry Vlll - aided by Gutenberg's press, spread all over Europe the new thinking and teaching. There arose anti-Catholic upheavals, conflicts between individuals, families, nations, the results of which are still very extant among us.

There were born in the 1550's new structures of liberal and secular thought, as important as those which had formerly separated Western Civilisation from the Eastern, which in fact had guaranteed the increasing growth in importance of the West. The Separated Brethren no longer thought as the Catholic Church did, nor did they accept her traditions. They went their own way - faith in Jesus sufficing, with only the Bible as guide - ***sola fide*** and ***sola scriptura.***

(See Chap. 12 – The Reformation; Chap. 13 – Sola Scriptura; Chap. 14 – Sola Fide)

The groups started by these seven dissidents grew exponentially, and 500 years later there are now an estimated 47,000 non-Catholic sects world-wide, all differing, each contradicting the other, with a new one being born every few days. It is therefore clear that the Reformation experiment seems to have failed, there being no central authority to hold these groups together, nor is there any consensus in their beliefs, many of whom are merely nominally Christian.

At this moment, the former Christian Europe has become post-Christian Europe, and the Reformation has influenced terribly the Church itself. Young Catholics have lost contact with their roots, many know Jesus only by hearsay, there being no personal relationship with Him. Families have broken up, vocations have plummeted, and except for the elderly, the Church is not a mother entrusted with the commission of Jesus to spread the Word. The essential life of the Church, the Sacraments, are but mere memory for many Catholic youth, as is their belonging to the Church in which they were baptised and, we surmise, confirmed. Cohabitation has overtaken the Sacrament of Catholic Marriage. (See <u>Chap. 20 – The Catholic Family</u>)

For the young of the Separated Brethren, the situation is no better. Their adults have mostly ceased to practice, and as with Catholic youth, many young people have turned to drugs and delinquency. In general, there is an abysmal ignorance about their religion, their history, and what God expects of them. The original Reformers having rejected the Sacraments of the Church, seeing them mainly as symbols, it is not surprising that their young do the same - when they hear about them.

(See <u>Chap. 1 – The Divine Plan</u>; <u>Chap. 18 – Jesus' Presence</u>)

What is perhaps the saddest result, is that Jesus himself for many has become only a symbol of good, of an unrealised dream. <u>As he is now in fact a mere symbol</u>, not a real Person on whom they can rely, in whom they can trust, there is a crying need today for a substantial re-heating of the message of Jesus, both in the Catholic Church and in the churches of the Brethren, for Jesus had warned

**"When the Son of Man comes, will he find any faith on earth?"
(Lk.18:8)**.

>How shall the young remain sinless?
>By obeying your word.
>I have sought you with all my heart:
>Let me not stray from your commands.
>I treasure your promise in my heart,
>Lest I sin against you.
>Blessed are you, O Lord;
>Teach me your commands
>(Ps. 118(119), vs. 9-12)

-o-o-o-o-o-o-o-

CHAPTER 3
The WORD

Words from the WORD

An old proverb tells us *"Sticks and stones may break my bones, but words can never harm me"*. Really? Is that so?

This old proverb may be correct in some ways, but quite incorrect in others, because words can be either harmless, consoling and loving, encouraging, or totally hateful and devastating. Words form an intimate part of our human existence, without them we risk becoming non-communicative, inhuman, robotic. And how can normal human beings reasonably communicate with non-humans or robots? Today's technology is doing a lot of research on Artificial Intelligence (A.I.), but although much has facilitated robot-human communication, yet a lot remains to be done, above all on the emotional level, e.g. can a robot experience grief, love, or other human emotions? Secularism considers this to be reasonable thinking.

On the biblical level, the art of communication has been taken to completely different and higher levels. The 46 books of the Tanakh [the Old Testament] is the history of the Jews, of their origins as the little tribe of the Epiru from the south of Baghdad in Iraq, its episodes of slavery (in Egypt and Babylon), its conquests of the Promised Land under Joshua, its religion starting from the covenants with Abraham, Moses, its expectations of a Messiah through the 16 books of prophecy. All this history was expounded through the words communicated to them from Yahweh [YHWH], and through their intense literacy programmes, using human words. Without these, there would never have been any Old Testament.

There is no difference either in the New Testament. It is a collection of revelatory words, every one of them turning around the Person and acts of Jesus the Christ, who many times claimed to be the expected Messiah, the Anointed, the very fulfilment of the ancient prophecies (**Mt.5:17-18**). Jesus proves that he is a master of the use of words, but what does he tell us about himself, his character, his message? He claimed divinity many times, using words in such a way as to make his hearers think (**Mt.12:8**; **Lk.1:22**). Speaking to his Apostles, he gives the strongest confirmation of his character. To Thomas who asks for the way to go to Jesus' destination, he replies **"I am the Way, the Truth, and the Life"** (**Jn.14:5-7**). These words of Jesus must be carefully examined, each word on its own merits.

"*I am*" is just one of the many times that Jesus refers to his divinity (**Jn.8:58**; **Mk.14:62**, referring to **Ex.3:13-15**). In this, he uses the words **"I AM WHO AM"** a use reserved solely to the High Priest during the sacrifices in the Temple, but he applies it to himself. Considered as blasphemy by his hearers, they tried to stone him (**Jn.8:59**), but he eluded them.

Of the three other characters, "Truth" is the most important, as it is by *"Truth"* that one finds the *"Way"* that leads to *"Life"*, all of which concepts belong exclusively to Jesus.

If therefore Jesus is the very Truth, the veracity of which belongs to God alone, then everything and every word he taught during his ministry must obligatorily be taken as the very expression of God's will. For instance, his teachings about love for one's enemies (**Lk.6:27-35**), of being compassionate (**Lk.6:36-38**), of prayer in secret (**Mt.6:5-6**), of forgiving others (**Mt.6:14-15**; **18:21-22**), of fasting (**Mt.6:16-18**; **Mk.2:18-22**; **Lk.5:33-39**), of not judging (**Mt.7:1-5**), of not fearing opposition to the message (**Mt.10:26-33**), of prayer in common (**Mt.18:19-20**), of treating others as one would like to be treated (**Mt.7:12**; **22:39**), of purity in marriage (**Mt.19:1-9**; **Mk.10:1-12; Lk.16:18**), must all be taken seriously.

Jesus warns his hearers against mere belief in him, who may consider themselves to be saved thereby. He stresses that faith must be bolstered by <u>active obedience</u> to the will of the Father (**Mt.7:21-27**). Obviously, the mere <u>presumption</u> of being saved by faith is unacceptable to Jesus, and to think otherwise would make his teaching just opinions, his warning useless. Even the Psalmist had uttered a prayer to avoid this. He says in **Ps.18(19) v.13**:

> From presumption restrain your servant
> And let it not rule me;
> Then I shall be blameless,
> Clean from grave sin.

All that Jesus taught were examples of his authoritative creation of new ways of thinking, of new thought structures, concerning oneself, others, life, God, eternity, et al. His teaching was quite unlike that of the ruling hierarchy of the scribes and doctors of the Law, who defended themselves by opinions and discussions among their peers, buttressing their teachings by quotations from the Scriptures and tradition.

On many occasions Jesus used certain words which were meant to impress the seriousness of his teaching. In the four Gospels he used *"I tell you"* eleven times, *"I tell you again"* once, *"I tell you truly"* twice, *"But I say to you"* nine times, and *"I tell you solemnly"* forty-five times. These phrases were used particularly in questions of morality or faith. Today's liberal thinking may complain that this is too dogmatic, but when it concerns an unalterable truth, one cannot compromise with half-truths or airy-fairy thinking. When Jesus gives a norm, it's a question of take-it or leave-it, nothing more, and nothing less.

It is evident that the totally new concepts of thought proposed by Jesus not only impressed certain hearers (**Mt.21:23-27**), but also caused serious opposition among many who were unable to accept them, thus fulfilling the prophecy of Isaiah (**Is.53:1**). Yet Isaiah had prophesied in God's name (***Is.45:23*** *– "By my own self I swear it, what comes from my mouth is truth, a word irrevocable"*). This was later clarified by **Is.55:11** *– "So the word that goes from my mouth does not return to me empty, without carrying out my will and succeeding in what it was sent to do"*.

Jesus often refers to himself as being sent by the Father, being taught by the Father, and as obeying his will (**Mt.11:27**; **Lk.10:22**; **Jn.8:49, 55d**; **10:17, 18d, 30, 37**), and this was further clarified by the Gospel of St John.

Who, or What, is Jesus, in fact?

Being the oldest and longest-living Apostle, John had had ample time to meditate on Jesus, his Incarnation, his being, his message. In **Jn.1:1-18** he shows clearly that Jesus is of divine origin, the very **word** of God foretold by Isaiah (**Jn.1:1-5**), the **word** who is "The true light that enlightens all men" (**Jn.1:9**), and that this **word** [from God] had taken human nature (**Jn.1:14** - was made flesh).

These were among the considerations taken into account in the deliberations of the Church concerning Jesus, and finally declared as doctrine that Jesus had a **dual nature**, i.e. his human nature was joined to his divine nature by the **hypostatic union** (*Council of Chalcedon, 451 AD). (See Chap.8 – Transubstantiation)

He is therefore the very **WORD** sent forth from the "mouth of God", with a mission to perform, and will return to the Father once this mission is accomplished (**Jn.19:30**).

Many biblical texts speak of someone called the "High Priest", e.g. in **Gen 14**, and in the letter to the Hebrews, written after the Resurrection, where Jesus is referred to as the "High Priest" several times. *"It was essential that he should in this way become completely like his brothers….to be a compassionate and trustworthy High Priest of God's religion* (**Heb.2:17**), *being able to help others in temptation, as he had been tempted".* Jesus is *"the apostle and High Priest of our religion"* (**Heb.3:1**). *"Since in Jesus, we have the supreme High Priest who has gone through to the highest heaven, we must never lose the faith that we have professed* (**Heb.4:14-15**), who is *"without sin".* (**Heb.7:26-28**) – *"The Law appoints weak men to be High Priests, but the promise on oath, after the Law, appointed the Son, who is made perfect for ever".*

Although being High Priest, the **WORD** was finally betrayed and brought before the Jewish Sanhedrin and Pilate the Governor. To this latter he answered to a question, ***"I came into the world to bear witness to the truth"***. *"Truth?"*, said Pilate, *"what is that?"* (**Jn.18:37-38**). The pagan Roman could not ever accept that Truth itself (physical and incarnate) was there before him, so even though he found no fault in the Man, he finally ceded to the Jewish demands and delivered him up for crucifixion (**Jn.19:16**).

Jesus the Truth was aware that eventually he would come to this, and had forewarned his Apostles three times about his betrayal his condemnation, suffering and death, and had foretold that he would rise again (**Mt.16:21**; **17:23**; **20:17-19**). Even though he knew that there would be opposition and persecution, yet he had prophesied *"Heaven and earth will pass away, but my words will never pass away"* (**Lk.21:33**).

Although they may accept Jesus as the Truth of the Almighty, as well as the eternal inalterability of his words, many not of the Catholic persuasion still have to explain just why they reject certain words and concepts used by him during his ministry.

Among several others, there follow three examples of rejection:

1) (**Mt.16:13-20**) – Following Simon's profession of faith, Jesus founds his Church, giving Simon a new name, "Peter" [the Rock]. Many claim that this is non-historical, which is patently absurd, considering the Church's history, from the approximate date of its foundation (33AD), and its continuing existence against all obstacles, to this year of 2020.

(See Chap. 16 – The Rock).

2) (**Jn.6:53-58** – completed **by Mt.26:26-29**, **Mk.14:22-25**, **Lk.22:19-20**, and **1Cor.11:23-30**) – The Real Presence of Jesus in the Eucharist has been a continuous belief of the Catholic Church from its beginnings to this very year of 2020, but has been considered to be a symbol only from the 16th century by the "Reformers".

(See Chap. 8 – Transubstantiation; Chap. 18 – Jesus' Presence)

3) (**Jn.20:21-23**) – This occurs in the evening of the very Day of his Resurrection (Easter Sunday), not quite the moment to joke or to offer inanities! The Resurrected Jesus passes through

the locked doors of the room where the disciples were hiding, fearful of the Jewish authorities. He, who had several times had forgiven the sins of others, for which he had been accused of blasphemy (**Mt.9:1-8**; **Lk.5:17-25, 7:36-50**; **Jn.8:1-12**), now goes one major step further. Before his crucifixion and death, he had formerly given to his disciples the privilege of curing the sick and of expulsing demons (**Mt.10:1**), but now he actually delegates his own divine power of forgiving the sins of others, and intends them to use this privilege with the gift of the Holy Spirit. Sins forgiven by them in the manner intended by him are in fact forgiven; but sins not forgiven – for one reason or another - are retained. (See Chap.18 – Jesus' Presence)

Jesus here has put into operation the psychological need of a penitent human to hear in human terms the forgiveness of his sins, which would give him the needed relief, backed up by the authority received from Christ himself. Could one ask for more? Or is one entitled to deny him the authority to delegate his own authority? (**Mt.16:13-20**)

However, it is now debatable that, if by merely asking the Almighty to forgive one's sins, without using the form delegated by Jesus to his disciples, they are thereby forgiven. Not that one should ever deny the grace of God in any circumstance, even in one such as this, but it seems that certainty should take precedence to uncertainty. A judge cannot judge himself in his own case, nor can a penitent – even a priest - forgive himself by the mere presumption of being forgiven. This would be auto-justification, in anyone's language.

Q: How did Jesus pass through doors, locked through fear of the Temple police (**Jn.7:32,45-47**)? **Ans**: *In passing through doors, he shows that his risen-glorified body is under the full control of his will and spirit. All matter is now subject to his spirit's control. Nothing,* *neither cloth, wood nor stone, can now retain him, nor can distance nor location.* (See Chap.10 – Resurrection proof).

*The Council of Chalcedon [451 AD] issued the Chalcedonian Definition, which repudiated the notion of a single nature in Christ, and declared that he has two natures in one Person and hypostasis. It also insisted on the completeness of his two natures: Godhead and manhood.

>
> Is the inventor of the ear unable to hear?
> The creator of the eye unable to see?
> The punisher of the pagans unable to punish?
> Yahweh the teacher of mankind
> Knows exactly how men think,
> How their thoughts are a puff of wind!
> (Ps.94:9-11)

-o-o-o-o-o-o-o-

CHAPTER 4
The Covenants

The Old – and the New

A Covenant, in biblical thinking, is not another name for a legal contract, which is in fact a sealed agreement between two parties. It is a free and explicit promise by God to someone. As means of unity or protection, covenants were always in use among the nations of ancient times, examples of which abound in the researches of anthropologists and museums. In the Old Testament there are several which are part of revealed holy history, and which in fact are fulfilled by the New Covenant of Jesus in the New Testament. Both of these types are shown below.

The Old Testament covenants

1) The Covenant with Noah after the Flood (**Gen.9:7-17**) – God promises that no more floods shall cover the earth, that Noah and his family will multiply and fill the earth, that the rainbow shall be sign of this everlasting covenant. No sacrifice of blood was used to seal this promise, it was by pure gratuity that it was made by God in Noah's favour.

2) The Covenant with Abram (**Gen.15:7-11**) – a sacrifice of blood was necessary; his name was changed to Abraham. To prove his trustworthiness, he was asked to sacrifice his son Isaac, but at the last moment a ram was provided and offered to God as seal of the covenant.

3) The Covenant with Moses (**Gen. 19-24**) – enacted after the liberation from slavery in Egypt. The Decalogue (the 10 Commandments) was given at Mount Sinai, and sacrifices of animals were made as sign of the Covenant (**Gen.24:5-8**). The Law of Moses (the Torah, the five books of Moses – Genesis, Exodus, Leviticus, Numbers, Deuteronomy) contain detailed instructions about rites and the ways to keep the terms of the covenant alive.

4) The Covenant with David (**2Sam.7:12-16**) – A promise that a descendant of David would be born, who would have a royal throne secure forever. On his deathbed he made his son Solomon swear to continue his work which he had begun, so that Yahweh's promise would be fulfilled (**1Kings 2:3-9**).

5) The Covenant with Jeremiah (**Jer.31:31-34**) – made when Israel had been divided into two kingdoms. Yahweh promises Jeremiah that he will make a new covenant with Israel, whose sin will be forgiven. Yahweh will be their God and they will be his people.

The New Testament Covenant

On the death of David's son Solomon, the Davidic dynasty of kings ended. The kingdom fell into schism of two kingdoms, Judah and Israel, and a series of kings of other families succeeded. After 381 years the schism ended, but was followed by Persian, Greek, and Roman occupations. During the Roman occupation

Jesus was born of the Davidic line, to which both Joseph and Mary belonged (**Lk.2:1-5**). He ministered for three years, mainly among his own people, and at the Last Supper, which happened the night before his crucifixion and death at Golgotha on Good Friday, he instituted two Sacraments, both of which go together.

1) **Sacrament of the Holy Eucharist.** <u>Over the bread</u>, Jesus [the High Priest] says *"Take this, all of you, and eat of it, for this is my Body, which will be given up for you"*. [This recalls the lamb sacrificed while preparing to leave Egyptian slavery (**Ex.12:8-14**); this became the Jewish Feast of Passover. Jesus is the true Lamb of God (**Jn.1:29,35**), sacrificed for all. Holy Mass is indeed a sacrifice, but an unbloody one, until the end of all time. If in a "state of grace", we may receive his Body in Holy Communion].

<u>Over the chalice with wine</u>, he then says *"Take this, all of you, and drink from it, for this is the chalice of my Blood, the Blood of the <u>new and eternal Covenant</u>, which will be poured out for you and for many, for the forgiveness of sins"*. [If in a "state of grace", and if permitted, we may also partake at the chalice]

(<u>This new covenant was instituted as a eternal fulfilment of the covenants of the Old Testament</u>. Also, after his Resurrection, Jesus appeared to his Apostles and delegated his own power to forgive sins (**Jn.20:21-23**), something to which he alone was privileged (**Mk.2:7-8**; **Lk.5:20-21**). This privilege is associated to the <u>Sacrament of Order</u>, the priesthood, as priests alone are permitted to forgive penitents. (See <u>Chap. 3 – The</u> **WORD**)

2) **Sacrament of Orders**. Having consecrated the bread and wine, transubstantiated into his Body and Blood, Jesus then gives a <u>command</u> to his Apostles, *"Do this in memory of me"* (**Lk.22:18**; **1Cor.11:23-30**).

[*This has been understood from the beginning of the Catholic Church to have been the inauguration of the new priesthood, which has now taken the place of the Jewish priests of the Old Testament.* <u>**There is no Jewish priesthood today**</u>. *According to the Old Testament, the only place from which it was appropriate to offer animal sacrifices to God was the Temple in Jerusalem. In A.D. 70 the Second Temple was destroyed, meaning Jewish priests no longer had a place to sacrifice. Since the Temple has been ruined, there is currently no place for sacrifice. Therefore, there is no active priesthood in Judaism*].

<u>To understand the **command "Do this in memory of Me"**</u>:

To **"Do"** means to perform this rite exactly as Jesus did, to not differ or change in any way, using the same physical elements used by him, unleavened bread and wine, not biscuits and/or soda-pop.

"This" is the command to use the same words and actions as he did.

"In memory" is not merely a simple recalling of the actions used at the Last Supper, it is a physical prolongation into the future for a perpetual re-actualisation of this **'new and eternal covenant'** for the salvation of the world.

"Of me" is to understand and realise that it is Jesus himself who is present at the Sacrifice of the Mass, using the agency of his priest to do the necessary sacrifice for the People of God. The human priest shares in the Priesthood of Jesus the God-man when he offers in unbloody sacrifice the bread and wine, which will become the very Body and Blood of Our Lord and Saviour.

The Catholic Priesthood

By the authority of the Catholic Church, and the delegated power to "bind and loose" (**Mt.16:19**), the Church has decided for many centuries that the priest is normally entitled to celebrate five of the seven Sacraments of the Church – Baptism, Reconciliation (Pardon), Marriage, Blessing of the Sick, and above all the Holy Eucharist, celebrated during Holy Mass. It is by this latter Sacrament that the ***New and Eternal Covenant of Jesus*** with his people is realised, to the "end of the age" (**Mt.28:18-20**).

If delegated by the Bishop of the diocese, the priest can also celebrate that of Confirmation, the strengthening of the newly baptised person for the witness he should give to the truths of the Faith he is called to profess.

However, he is not entitled to celebrate the Sacrament of Orders, the ordaining of new priests, which is reserved to Bishops alone. The priest can be present at the ceremony of ordination, to bless the newly ordained by the laying-on of hands, another ancient rite of the Church.

Although separated from the western Catholic Church since 1054 AD, the Orthodox Church(es) also has/have a valid priesthood, whereas the various denominations of the Separated Brethren have merely ministers in their service. Having denied the Sacrament of Orders, among other doctrines which are also denied, their ministers are not priests, and this includes those of the Anglican Communion, which itself is very divided over these issues.

> *O God, you are my God, for you I long,*
> *For you my soul is thirsting.*
> *My body pines for you*
> *Like a dry, weary land without water.*

John Boos M.Afr

So I gaze on you in the sanctuary
To see your strength and your glory.
(Ps. 62(63), vs. 1-2)

-o-o-o-o-o-o-o-

CHAPTER 5
The Incarnation

Definition and Heresies

Given the importance of this subject, it is necessary to give its background. All the Prophets of ancient Israel had spoken about the coming of a Messiah, but it was Micah (**Mi.5:1-4**), Ezekiel, who had promised a Messiah-Shepherd (**Ez.34:1-34**), and Isaiah whose words are most relevant (**Is.7:14**) concerning the coming Messiah. The child would be born of a maiden in Bethlehem, which occurred between 7 – 4 BC, (not at the connecting point between BC and AD, due to the incorrect calculations of the monk Denys). The child Jesus grew up in Nazareth with his mother Mary and foster-father Joseph. Arrived at manhood, he ministered for three years, was condemned to death on spurious charges of sedition and blasphemy, and was crucified and entombed in Jerusalem. He rose as he had promised, appeared several times to his Apostles, and commanded them to proclaim his message to the world. He then ascended to heaven, and according to his promise, will return to judge the living and the dead. Briefly, such is his story.

The one Church he had founded on Simon the Fisherman (**Mt.16:13-20**) grew and prospered, but there were always those who wished to know more about this Jesus. Who was he really? What was his nature? Was it true what the Church taught about him? What really was his message? These questionings went on for centuries, (are still continuing today!), and have given rise to many conflicting ideas about him. Many of these ideas are heresies, most being in some way an attack against the prime claim of **the Catholic-Christian Faith, that Almighty God became man in the Person of Jesus Christ.** The subject of this paper is to clarify all this, as it took centuries for the Church to bring into full view the truth about Our Lord.

Even before the Church had become well known, there had been many warnings against leaving its teaching to follow others. Here are some samples of such warnings:

Mt.7:15 – [Jesus] ***"Beware of false prophets, who come to you in sheep's clothing, but underneath are ravenous wolves".***

Mt.7:21-23 – [Jesus] ***"Not everyone who says to me 'Lord, Lord', will enter the kingdom of heaven, but only the one who does the will of my Father in heaven".*** [[*Faith is not enough, action (works) is also necessary*]]

Rm.16:17-18 – [Paul] *"I urge you, brothers, to watch out for those who create dissensions and obstacles, in opposition to the teaching that you learned; avoid them………they deceive the hearts of the innocent".*

2 Tim.4:3-4 – [Paul] *"The time will come when people will not tolerate sound doctrine but, following their own desires and itching ears, will accumulate teachers and will stop listening to the truth, and will follow myths".*

Acts 20:29-30 – [Paul] – *"When I am gone, fierce wolves will invade you and will have no mercy on the flock….with a travesty of truth on their lips to induce the disciples to follow them".*

2 Pet. 2:1-2 – [Peter] *"There will be false teachers among you, who will introduce destructive heresies and even deny the Master who ransomed them. They will destroy themselves very quickly".*

Heb.13:9 - *"Do not let yourselves be carried away by all kinds of strange doctrines".*

Having had to fight for its life and teachings against the early heresies (some are detailed below), and Roman persecutions, the Church had been obliged to live underground, in the extensive cemeteries (catacombs) around Rome, and was only able to become public in 313 AD, when the Emperor Constantine published his Edict of Toleration. It was only then that she was able to decide on the authenticity of the texts offered as worthy of being included in the Bible, and this the early Fathers and Councils did – Muratorian Canon (200 AD), St. Athanasius (367 AD), Pope Damasus (382 AD), St. Jerome (382-405 AD), Council of Hippo (393 AD), 1st Council of Carthage (397 AD), Pope St. Innocent (405 AD), 2nd Council of Carthage (419 AD). These early findings were reaffirmed by the Councils of Florence (1441 AD), Trent (1546), and Vatican 1 (1869).

The **Council of Chalcedon (451 AD),** had a lot to define about Jesus, considering the many heresies then circulating, the greatest of them concerning his very nature. Due to the Virgin Mary's having accepted to become the mother of the Son of God at the Angel's invitation (**Lk.1:26-38**), Jesus had, from the very instant of her acceptance (his conception) and his subsequent gestation in her womb, possessed two (***dual***) natures, human and divine, which would form part of his daily life afterwards. Thus, the Catholic Church teaches that *Jesus is both human and divine.*

In his public life, Jesus would use his **human nature** to teach, according to human understanding, (**Mt.5:1-48**; **Mk.3:22-30**; **Lk.11:1-13**; **Jn.5:19-47**). His humanity would also have need of nourishment (**Mk.11:12-14**), repose (**Mt.8:23-25**), human companionship (**Mt.4:18-22**), and he would show impatience and frustration (**Mt.16:1-4**), anger (**Mt.21:12-14**), and many other attitudes plainly attributable to a human being.

Jesus would also use his **divine nature** to heal the physically sick with merely a word, which God alone can do (**Mt.9:27-34**; **Mk.3:1-6**; **Lk.7:1-10**; **Jn.9:1-41**); to forgive sinners, the spiritually sick (**Mt.9:1-8**; **Mk.2:1-6**; **Lk.23:39-43**; **Jn.8:3-11**); to control nature (**Mt.8:23-27**; **Mk.6:30-44**; **Lk.9:12-17**; **Jn.6:5-13**); to raise the dead (**Mt.9:23-26**; **Mk.5:35-43**; **Lk.7:11-17**; **Jn.11:28-44**). It is clear that these astounding acts could be accomplished only by God himself.

Notwithstanding these decisions of the Council of Chalcedon and others, there were many who just could not accept their decisions, and thus have entered into heresy. A heresiarch is the founder of a heresy, those who follow, mainly through ignorance, brainwashing, or plain adamancy, are also technically considered as being heretical, but with different degrees of culpability, according to the use of their free will to follow the said erroneous doctrine. But what really is a heresy? And why is the Incarnation the object of their constant attention and attacks?

A heresy, in the religious context, is an *"Opinion or doctrine contrary to the orthodox tenets of a religious body or church"* (Collins English Dictionary), although the term may be applied also to scientific, economic, social or political theories. The following are the principal heresies against the Catholic faith. All of these in some way, whether concerning the human or divine natures of Our Lord, or both, were/are opposed the Catholic Church's teaching of Jesus, subject of the Incarnation.

N.B: *the following are the merest sketchings of the heresies mentioned. There are voluminous writings on each, but those are reserved to specialists in this important field of religious study.*

c. 75-90 AD – Cerinthus of Rome and his followers denied the divinity of Jesus. St John the Evangelist countered this by using the Greek word "Logos" ("Word") in his Gospel. This word means "an emanation from a source, absolutely indistinguishable from the original source", the source being divine, God himself, (**Jn.1:1-3, 14**). Thus, the "**WORD**" is God Himself. The heresy of Cerinthus died a natural death, as people came to understand the importance of the Gospel.

140 AD – Marcion, an anti-Semitic Roman businessman, rejected Jesus' Jewishness. He believed in two gods, rejecting the "cruel" God of the Old Testament, Yahweh, but accepting the good God, Abba, of the New. Jesus was not of the divine nature of Abba; he was only merely human. Marcionism was absorbed by Manicheanism, and died out eventually.

c. 250-270 AD - Manicheanism – founded by Mani, an Iranian "prophet". For him, all matter was evil, spirit alone mattered. Jesus' humanity therefore was evil, being of matter. This eventually died out, but St. Augustine was for some time involved in its teachings. This heresy was followed by the Cathars (see below).

c. 235-375 AD - Arianism - due to Arius, Patriarch of Constantinople. He held that Jesus had been an extra-ordinary human being, but was only human, not divine. This was condemned by the Council of Nicaea, 325 AD.

411 AD – Pelagianism, founded by the monk Pelagius. He denied Original Sin and God's grace, believing that Original Sin did not taint human nature, and that free will could achieve human perfection, without grace. Thus, he denied that Jesus' work of redeeming mankind was necessary. This was condemned by the Council of Ephesus, 431 AD.

420 – 525 AD – Semi-Pelagianism. This taught that human will sufficed, that grace could be merited by human effort, and that once justified, the person would be saved. This was condemned by the Councils of Orange, 529 AD, and Trent, 1546.

420 AD to today, with HQ in Chicago, USA – Nestorianism. This began with Nestorius, Patriarch of Constantinople, who objected to the title of Mother of God **(Theotokos)** given to Mary, mother of Jesus, by the 3rd Council of Ephesus, 431 AD. According to Nestorius, Jesus was fully human, not divine, so Mary could not be given the title "Mother of God". This was condemned by the Council of Chalcedon, 451 AD. This heresy was very axed to missionary life; it went to the Arabian Peninsula, was influential in the start of Islam, and also went to China, where tombs and memorial plaques have been found.

c.550 + - Monophysitism – a belief that Jesus was really divine, his humanity was only a disguise. This complicated and important heresy still exists, and can be found in the non-Chalcedonian churches of the East – the Copts being foremost.

860s AD – Photianism. From Photius, a layman quickly ordained priest and consecrated as Patriarch of Constantinople. Soon deposed, he accused the Western Church of heresy for having inserted the *"filioque"* ("and from the Son") in the Creed without discussion and acceptance by the Eastern Church. This means that Jesus did not send the Spirit to mankind, as he had promised (<u>Jn.16:7</u>), thus implying that Jesus was not divine. This was not an important heresy, but a schism, brought to a head in 1054, from which the Orthodox Churches claim their existence. This has not as yet been healed.

<u>12th – 14th centuries</u> – the <u>Cathars</u> from southern France, parts of Spain and Italy. (aka Albigensians, from Albi, one of their main towns). This was a gnostic sect with belief in two gods, a good creator and an evil one of matter. It came from the Manichean heresy [above]. The Cathars considered themselves "purists", and almost all of the mediaeval Church's teachings were rejected, especially those concerning Jesus. Sex as recreation was encouraged, marriage was not. The Cathars practised abortion and birth control, and believed in reincarnation. A State government and Church crusade was launched against them in 1209, and there were many massacres. This sect died out gradually, but continued in hiding for many years.

<u>1517 – present day</u> – the <u>Reformation</u>. [See <u>Chaps.12 – 14</u> for further information and analysis]. Basically, <u>the said Reformers and their followers</u>, while accepting the dual natures of Jesus Our Lord – <u>Council of Chalcedon 451 AD</u> – and while insisting on the literal interpretation of ***sola scriptura*** as their *raison d'etre* of being saved (which by their very admission had condemned to eternal hell all those who for the preceding 1520 years had had only the Catholic Church to expound Jesus' message), <u>had decided</u>, quite illogically and contradicting their own precepts, <u>not to take literally the words of Jesus in the Gospels</u> (See <u>Chap. 3 – The **WORD**</u>). This heresy was condemned by the <u>Council of Trent, 1546-1563</u>.

17th century – Jansenism, from C. Jansen, Bishop in France (+1638). From a twisted interpretation of St Augustine's teachings on grace, this heresy taught that Christ died only for the 'elect', the 'pure', those who lived a rigorous moral life in relation to the Sacraments. It also rejected man's free will and his ability to cooperate with God's grace. It was condemned by Popes Innocent X (1653) and Clement Xl (1713). This heresy has caused lasting problems for the Church, to this day.

Modern heresies – In some way, these are amalgamations or spin-offs from those of the past. Thus, the New Age came from the old pagan nature-cults of Osiris, Ra, Anubis etc. Madame Blavatsky founded it in the 1800's, giving rise to several sub-groups, basing themselves on theosophy, occultism, hallucinating drugs, crystals etc., but has always remained a sub-culture in society. Secularism is a spin-off from modernistic philosophies, and has gained popularity in former value-full societies which have lost the clarity of their values, and are now determined to eradicate any trace of those which remain. Those two are against all revealed and organised faiths, and not only against the Incarnation, as shown above.

Examples of attacks against the Incarnation follow:

Mt.16:13-20 – Jesus founds his one Church on Peter, who receives the title of "Rock". (See Chap.16 – The Rock). The Reformation refuses the visible Church of Jesus confided to fallible humans, considering it non-historic, amorphous. This is an attack against the dual natures of Jesus, both of which were here in action.

Jn.6:53-56 – <u>Jesus gives his radical Discourse on the Bread of Life</u> to the people in the synagogue of Capernaum, saying that it is necessary to eat his body and drink his blood to attain eternal life. Many leave, scandalised, just as followers of the Reformers have done, who have interpreted his words only symbolically. <u>This is an attack against the human nature of Jesus</u>, who speaks quite literally for the people to understand.

Mt.26:26-29; **Mk.14:22-23**; **Lk.22:19-20**; **1Cor.11:23-27** – <u>The Institution of the Holy Eucharist</u> at the Last Supper, the importance of which cannot be over-emphasised. The Reformers consider it merely symbolic, doubting the words of Jesus, thus <u>this is an attack against his divine nature</u>, he having performed an act attributable solely to God, and is also a refusal of his inauguration of the Priesthood ("***Do this in memory of Me***"). The Sacrament of the Priesthood is exclusive to Catholics and Orthodox. (cf. <u>Chap.4 – The Covenants</u>).

Jn.20:21-23 - After the Resurrection, <u>Jesus delegates his authority to forgive sins</u>, something which only God can do, which he himself had done on several occasions, (**<u>Lk.5:18-25</u>**; **<u>Jn.8:3-11</u>**). Jesus here is eliminating the belief held by non-Catholic groups that one can go straightaway to God to ask pardon for sins, as here he gives them his preferred method. Unfortunately, the Separated Brethren prefer to go to God alone. Basically, this means forgiving oneself, a form of auto-justification, which ultimately leads to <u>Presumption</u>. <u>This attacks Jesus' divine nature, through</u> **Doubt** and **Scepticism**. (See <u>Chap.18 – Jesus' Presence</u>).

Insofar as the literal words of Jesus are denied (as above), and are construed only symbolically, not as a <u>delegation of authority belonging solely to his divine nature</u>, the "Reformers", and all subsequent groups, denominations and sects, can be seen to have officially attacked the Incarnation, although this may not have been their intention. Attacked also are all subsequent conclusions stemming from the Incarnation, which the Church has defined through the centuries. Most Protestants are ignorant of these conclusions, or are unwilling to investigate, satisfied to remain as they have been for some time. The very idea of investigating their faith is abhorrent to them, and relatively few have returned to their roots, notwithstanding the great efforts of the Ecumenical Movement.

DOUBT, or **SCEPTICISM,** is probably the determining reason for the attacks against the Incarnation. It is one of the foremost qualities of the human being, by which one asserts one's own identity and reinforces the value of one's self-esteem. Without doubt there is no possible place for any advancement in science, politics, sociology, and particularly in religion. Thomas, the Apostle who doubted the fact of the Resurrection of Jesus, even when assured by his companions, put his own empirical and 'scientific' character foremost (for which he has received the sobriquet of "Doubting Thomas"), and was convinced only when he had tactile experience of the wounds in the body of Jesus himself (**Jn.20:24-29**).

This quality – or weakness – of doubt, could possibly explain just why those groups which had followed the original Reformers, having lost the certainty of the "Peters" who have formed the chronological and historical line of Church leaders since 33AD, in just a few years had begun to break up and form new groups, each with its own justificatory teachings and reasonings, while still retaining the basic tenets of the Reformation – *sola scriptura* and *sola fide*, (see <u>Chaps. 13 & 14</u>).

Self-vindication is but poor defence, and there is still some need to explain just how, after only 500 years, the Reformation movement has given birth to **47,000 non-Catholic Christian sects around the world**, (according to the estimation of the 2018 Gordon-Conwell Evangelical Seminary in the US), many of which are only Christian by name, not by solid teaching.

Depending on each particular heresy, it is evident that, to a greater or lesser extent, each heresy had had doubts about the faith of its immediate and previous provenance, and this became a cornerstone of its own teaching. Thus, the Reformation groups had had doubts about the faith of the Catholic Church. Presbyterianism then learned from Calvinism, Anglicanism gave birth to the Congregationalists, Quakers, Methodists, Episcopalians, the Salvation Army, Pentecostalists, Four-Square Gospel churches, Adventists, Assemblies of God churches, etc etc, finally arriving at the unbelievably horrendous figure of sects above. Whether it were the Arians, the Nestorians, the Monophysites, the Manicheans, the Cathars, or whatever group coming from them, each group doubted that Jesus had literally meant what he had said, e.g. the foundation of the Church on Simon-Peter, the Eucharist, the inauguration of the Catholic Priesthood, the forgiveness of sins, and others.

Doubt is indeed a great reason for leaving a church and starting anew, but needs selective choosing - cherry-picking - of appropriate texts to support one's decisions. This can be seen only as a justified expression of an attitude of doubt, which leads to flight from a doctrine, which leads to another flight, and to another, and another, ….and this explains everything.

It is to be hoped that the gift of the Spirit, promised by Jesus in **Jn.16:12-15**, and actualised at Pentecost – 50 days after Easter (**Acts 2:1-13**) – will be repeated in some way, so that the promise of Jesus, that there would be **"one flock, and One Shepherd"**, (**Jn.10:16**) would be eventually realised. These unfortunate divisions have lasted long enough, but perhaps God had permitted them as a test of our faithfulness.

NB: *All the heresies above had had their beginnings <u>in Christendom itself</u>, but there are <u>two</u> which are <u>on the</u> <u>outside of the Catholic Faith</u>. Each will now be briefly summarised.*

Judaism

This is the very mother-lode of Christendom. The latter did not flee from the former, but considers itself to be the fulfilment of the Mosaic Law and the prophecies, based on the Person of Jesus, the Messiah. Judaism accepts Jesus only as a Jew, but, (except for the very few who have accepted the Faith), totally rejects his Messianic claims. Technically, this is an extra-Ecclesial heresy, and Judaism today does not concern itself with the Church Councils concerning Jesus the Christ whom, they say, had been "hanged on the tree" (Talmud).

Islam

This extra-Ecclesial heresy began in 632 AD, at the death of its "prophet", Muhammad. It started among poly-theistic Arabs, who worshipped the 365 deistic plaques in the Kaaba in Makkah. Islam was influenced by Zoroastrianism (Iran), Gnosticism (Rome and its environs), Hinduism, Greek and Roman gods (due to proximity), Judaism (with colonies in Arabia after 70AD, following the destruction of the Second Temple by the Roman forces), and heretical Nestorianism. <u>Concerning Jesus</u>, Islam followed particularly Arianism and Nestorianism, considering him an <u>extra-ordinary human being, but not divine</u>. Besides,

Jesus neither died on the Cross, nor did he rise again (Qur'an: Sura 5:147)

-o-o-o-o-o-o-o-

> How can I repay the Lord
> For his goodness to me?
> The cup of salvation I will raise;
> I will call on the Lord's name.
> My vows to the Lord I will fulfil
> Before all the people.
> A thanksgiving sacrifice I make,
> I will call on the Lord's name.
>
> (Ps.115(116), vs.12-14, 17)

-o-o-o-o-o-o-o-

CHAPTER 6
Humility

Its Most Absolute Expression

Humility is the quality of being **humble.** Humility, in various interpretations, is widely seen as a virtue which centers on low self-preoccupation, or unwillingness to put oneself forward. As it is found in many religious and philosophical traditions, it contrasts with narcissism, hubris, and other forms of pride, and is an idealistic and rare intrinsic construct that has an extrinsic side. The term "humility" comes from the Latin word *humilitas*, a noun related to the adjective *humilis*, which may be translated as "humble", but also as "grounded", or "from the earth", since it derives from *humus*, (earth). The word "humble" may be related to feudal England where the lowest cuts of meat, or 'umbles', that is to say whatever was left over when the "upper classes" had taken their parts, were provided to the lowest class of citizen. The term 'humble pie,' meaning to exist in a lowly station, may derive from this definition.

New Testament exhortations to humility are found in many places, for example *"Blessed are the gentle"* (**Mt. 5:4**), *"He who exalts himself will be humbled and he who humbles himself will be* *exalted"* (**Mt. 23:12**), as well as (**Phil. 2:5-8**), and in the Letter of James, especially **Jas.1: 19-27**, and **2:14-26**).

C, S. Lewis writes, in *Mere Christianity*, that pride is the "anti-God" state, the position in which the ego and the self are directly opposed to God: ***"Unchastity, anger, greed, drunkenness, and all that, are mere fleabites in comparison: it was through Pride that the angel [Lucifer] became the devil: Pride leads to every other vice: it is the complete anti-God state of mind"***. In contrast, Lewis contends that, in Christian moral teaching, the opposite of pride is humility.

"True humility" is distinctly different from "false humility" which consists of deprecating one's own sanctity, gifts, talents, and accomplishments for the sake of receiving praise or adulation from others, as personified by the fictional character Uriah Heep, created by Charles Dickens. In this present context, <u>legitimate humility</u> comprises the following behaviours and attitudes:

- Submitting to God and legitimate authority.
- Recognizing virtues and talents that others possess, particularly those that surpass one's own, and giving due honour and, when required, obedience.
- Recognizing the limits of one's talents, ability, or authority.

The vices most opposed to humility are: Pride, and a too great obsequiousness or abjection of oneself. Catholic texts view humility as annexed to the cardinal virtue of temperance. St Bernard defines it as***, "A virtue by which a man knowing himself as he truly is, abases himself. Jesus Christ is the ultimate definition of Humility"***. This last definition will now be examined.

It is the firm belief of most Christians, (excluding those of fringe groups who accept Jesus as Saviour but deny his divinity), that Jesus

Christ is the Son of the Almighty Father, promised through the ages by the *Jewish prophets and fulfilled by the Incarnation, life, teaching, death and Resurrection of this unique Person. Through the authority of the Church instituted by him (**Mt 16:13-20**), this has been clarified by the great Councils called throughout her history. At the risk of repetition, this Person, according to the Church's own definition, is God himself, the Second Person of the Most Blessed Trinity.

How can we possibly accept and understand that the Uncaused Cause of everything that exists or could exist, that the *"I AM WHO I AM"* of **Ex.3:13-15**, could possibly even consider becoming a lowly, mortal human being, taking unto himself the physical form of being, needing the alimentation and repose of normal humans, and to be subject to the other human beings of his time, and yet be sinless? (Cf. **Heb.4:15**; **2Cor.5:21**; **Gaudium et Spes** #22 (Vatican ll)

This is an attempt to clarify and define the problem, that of the humility of God.

Although all the Prophets had prophesied concerning the coming of the Messiah, Isaiah and Wisdom have their say here:

Is.45:23: *"By my own self I swear it, that which comes from my mouth is truth, a word irrevocable"*.

Is.55:11: *"So the word that goes from my mouth does not return to me empty, without carrying out my will, and succeeding in what it was sent to do"*.

Wisdom 18:15 – *"In peaceful silence….down from the heavens…..leapt your all-powerful Word…into a doomed land"*.

These prophecies were fulfilled by the coming of Jesus, whom St John has identified as the "**Word**" of God in **Jn.1:1-3** *"In the beginning was the Word: the Word was with God, and the Word was God. He was with God in the beginning. Through him all things came to be, not one thing had its being but through him"*. (See Chap. 3 – Incarnation, for "Logos")

In **Jn.1: 9** – *"The Word was the true light that enlightens all men"*:

In **Jn.1:14** – *"The Word was made flesh, he lived among us, and we saw his glory, the glory that is his as the only son of the Father, full of grace and truth"*. John personifies the Word as a human being.

NB: The word "**Word**" is not just an outward expression of thought. John uses the Greek "Logos", which itself is the divine wisdom manifested in the creation, government, and redemption of the world, an emanation indistinguishable from its divine source, God Himself; in Catholic theology **Word** is identified with the Second Person of the Blessed Trinity, the God-Man Jesus the Christ. (**Eph.1:3, 9-10; 2:4-6**).

The Councils of the Catholic Church for many centuries considered these ancient prophecies and gave their decisions - Council of Nicaea (325 AD), 2nd Council of Constantinople (381 AD), 3rd Council of Ephesus (431 AD) – these determined Jesus' fulfilment of the prophecies, his relationship to the Father, the role of the Holy Spirit, his founding of his Church.

Jesus had both divine and human natures, as decided by the Council of Chalcedon, 451 AD. This Council declared dogmatically that Jesus has **TWO NATURES**, one divine, the other human. This would mean that although *Jesus had all the* *attributes of a human being*, yet *he possesses also the "fullness of divinity in his body"* (**Col.2:9**). This would explain his need for food and rest, his fatigue, his need for companionship, his outbursts of impatience, the possibility of his death. These are human attributes, added to his corporeal stature, his voice, senses of sight, hearing, movement, etc.

His divinity would also be amply demonstrated by his many miracles and cures – some at a distance -, his raising of the dead to life, his unique methods of teaching (the parables, his Jewish humour (**Mt.7:3-5**), his causing the Jewish authorities to consider their own traditions and laws, his prophecies, the founding of his Church, and his Resurrection and Ascension). To cap it all, this very divinity accepted to be humiliated in the most excruciating and bloody sacrifice on the Cross.

> *He was humbled in the womb of the Virgin, needy in the manger of the sheep, homeless on the pathways of Palestine, friendless on the wood of the Cross.*
> *Nothing so humbles the proud sinner as the humility of Christ's humanity.* (St Anthony of Padua)

And yet, knowing that one day he would be betrayed and condemned to death, Jesus prepared to leave us a souvenir. Not a sandal or prayer-shawl, he chose to leave us his very self. In **Jn.6:35, 48** he states clearly *"I am the bread of life"*, and in **Jn.6:51** he continues *"I am the living bread which has come down from heaven. Anyone who eats this bread will live forever; and the bread that I shall give is my flesh, for the life of the world"*.

To those who argue and complain about this (**Jn.6:52**), he bravely continues, insisting, *"I tell you most solemnly, if you do not eat of the flesh of the Son of Man* [[**Dan.7:13-14**]], *and drink his blood, you will not have life in you"*;

Jn.6:55 – *"For my flesh is real food, and my blood is real drink. He who eats my flesh and drinks my blood lives in me, and I live in him"*;

Jn.6:54 – *"Anyone who does eat my flesh and drink my blood has eternal life, and I will raise him up on the last day"*;

Jn.6:58d – *"Anyone who eats this bread will live forever"*.

The souvenir he leaves will be his very Self, in the form of Bread.

To some of his listeners in the synagogue of Capernaum these words seemed outrageous and perhaps cannibalistic – contravening the laws of the Tanakh [Old Testament] itself (**Gn.1:26-27** – implying not to eat others made in God's image)

Many abandoned him (**Jn.6:66**), and he let them go, did not call them back. His words were rejected, as they are to this day by many who claim to believe in him, though not accepting his words literally, as he meant them to be understood.

But the Apostles stayed with him, he *"had the message of eternal life"* (**Jn.6:67-69**). It was to these men and to the Church of the future that Jesus left his personal souvenir. In **Mt.26:26-29**, **Mk.14:22-25**, and **Lk. 22:19-20**, Our Lord instituted the Eucharist of his Body [his flesh] and Blood, pronouncing his words over the bread and wine of the meal at the Last Supper, considered from earliest times to have been the First Mass.

This was repeated by St Paul in **1Cor.11:23-26**, coupled with the warning *"Everyone is to recollect himself before eating this Bread and drinking this Cup, because a person who eats and drinks without recognizing the Body is eating and drinking his own condemnation"*. The Church therefore teaches that anyone in a state of mortal (serious) sin should refrain from receiving Holy Communion until his/her situation is rectified by Confession, repentance, and forgiveness (**Jn.20: 21-23**).

Seemingly harsh words. But this decision stems from that of the Council of Chalcedon (451AD) already cited above, and must also be applied here.

As Our Lord is possessed of TWO NATURES – the divine and physically human – which continued throughout his life, then the very bread and wine of the meal, over which he has pronounced the words of Consecration ***"This is my Body... this is my Blood"***, (also pronounced over the offerings at every Mass from early days to this day), are by the words of Jesus and the very logical nature of things also possessed of TWO NATURES in themselves, both divine and physical.

The bread used has all the attributes of bread – composition, weight, colour, taste – and is absorbed into our bodies upon digestion. On the other hand, the Divinity present in the Eucharist is not absorbed as are the attributes of bread. On the contrary, the Divinity of Jesus absorbs the communicant into Itself - ***He who eats my flesh and drinks my blood lives in me, and I live in him*** (**Jn.6:56**). The [consecrated] wine itself also possesses all the attributes of ordinary wine (taste, colour, weight), yet it is the very Blood of Our Lord, reactualised, *"done in memory of Me"*, as He had expressly commanded.

This is the most extreme example of humility one could possibly imagine, that Almighty God, Creator and Sustainer of absolutely all existence, has not only humiliated himself to take upon himself our fallen and weak human nature, but now has humiliated himself to the extreme, and has become the most basic foods of human existence, bread, and wine.

Bethlehem = "House of Bread". Jesus was born in the animal enclosure of the inn in the little town of Bethlehem, as there was no place for them in the inn **(Lk.2:7)**. His foster-father Joseph had taken his child-bearing wife Mary there, so as to conform to the Roman order to register in the place where his ancestors had come from, as both were of the Davidic line. The great king David had been born of Jesse of Bethlehem (**1Sam.16:1-5**), but the line of kingship had died out. This association with Joseph and Mary means that Jesus would be considered as being born of the Davidic line himself.

Considering dispassionately the life of Jesus, it is clear that his entire life was offered as a gift to humanity – to his people, to the sick, to the Jewish hierarchy, and to the poor and despised. At the end of his life, he prepares his followers to accept his final gift – by the "Discourse on the Bread of Life" in Capernaum, (**Jn 6:32-58**), in the Cenacle (**Mt.26:26-29**, **Mk.14:22-25**, and **Lk. 22:19-20**), and by his promise to knock at the door, to enter and eat with us (**Rev.3:20**). His words in the Our Father "daily bread", (***"epi ousious"*** = daily supernatural Bread, *in Greek*) also inform us that he wishes this unbloody sacrifice to be a daily one, not only on the day of rest, as his Body and Blood are given daily in the Real Presence, for our supernatural benefit. This explains just why the Catholic Church celebrates Holy Mass daily, everywhere.

The Church not only believes in the actual Real Presence of God at all times in a valid Eucharist, but also why every Mass is a celebration, not just a service. This is not symbolism, and was never meant to be symbolism. It is Jesus himself who had promised **"I am with you always, even to the end of the age"** (**Mt 28:20**). He assures this in prayer, and in all the Sacraments, but especially in the mystery of the Sacred Eucharist, the very hub of all sanctity in the Church.

(See Chap.18 – Jesus' Presence)

Phil.2:6-11

Though he was in the form of God, Jesus did not count equality with God a thing to be grasped. He emptied himself, taking the form of a servant, being born in the likeness of men. And being found in human form, he humbled himself, and became obedient unto death, even death on a cross. Therefore, God has highly exalted him, and bestowed on him the name which is above every name; That at the name of Jesus every knee should bow, in heaven and on earth, and under the earth; and every tongue confess that Jesus Christ is Lord, to the glory of God the Father.

***The 4 Major Prophets** -Isaiah, Jeremiah, Ezekiel, Daniel.
***The 12 Minor Prophets** - Hosea, Joel, Amos, Obadiah, Jonah, Micah, Nahum, Habakkuk, Zephaniah, Haggai, Zechariah, Malachi.

> He has put into my heart a marvellous love
> For the faithful ones who dwell in his land.
> O Lord, it is you who are my portion and cup,
> It is you yourself who are my prize.
> The lot marked out for me is my delight,
> Welcome indeed the heritage that falls to me.

(Ps.15(16), vs. 3, 5-6)

-o-o-o-o-o-o-o-

CHAPTER 7
Didacticism

Biblical Didacticism

The Catholic Church considers the whole Bible as inspired, as the Word of God revealed through the centuries to the Chosen People at first in the Old Testament (OT), then to the Church in the New Testament (NT). Guaranteed by the inspiration of the Holy Spirit (**Jn.16:12-15**), she interprets through the centuries the will of God for humanity, by her *magisterium*, her teaching authority.

There are certain biblical events recounted, both in the OT and in the NT, in which no third person was present to record the event, but which are still regarded as inspired. The Church considers these events to have been used as teaching methods *before* the Church even existed, either by the early Jewish teachers (Priestly or Yahvistic groups), or by one of the writers of the NT. Such texts are seen to be ***didactic*** (teaching), with the aim of clarifying a situation or to encourage a series of actions. The following is intended to give examples of this method, but there are many others, the aim of which can be found by the interested seeker.

Didaktikos is a Greek word that means "apt at teaching." It comes from *didaskein,* meaning "to teach." Something "didactic" does just that: it teaches or instructs. "Didactic" conveyed that neutral meaning when it was first borrowed in the 17th century, and still does; a didactic piece of writing is one that is meant to be instructive as well as artistic. Parables are generally didactic, because they aim to teach a moral lesson. Something "didactic" is often overburdened with instruction to the point of being dull. Or it might be pompously instructive or moralistic.

Didacticism itself is a philosophy that adheres to the notion that texts should be instructional as well as entertaining. A **didactic** text is one that teaches and instructs, and originally, the idea was that learning should be done in an intriguing manner. Over time, the term **didactic** has taken on a negative connotation, as a text that seeks to instruct or teach is sometimes seen as dull or "preachy." But this system is still widely used by instructors to open the minds of small children or those of special needs, using comical drawings, puppets, dolls, or skits to do so.

The five "books of Moses" – Genesis, Exodus, Leviticus, Numbers, Deuteronomy, - the Torah, are now considered to have taken their final completed form during the time of the Jewish exile in Babylon, in or about 550 BC, but parts were contributed by other authors over the centuries. But still, most of the basic ideas go back to Moses.

Post-exilic ancient Jewish teachers of morality had recourse to didacticism in their efforts to teach proper morality to their people, recovering from Egyptian slavery, still suffering psychically from the 40-year sojourn in the Arabian deserts, and once again in exile. In fact, there probably was a lot of unbecoming behaviour by the early Jewish people, and much of this behaviour must have concerned general morality and sexual problems in particular. Examples of such behaviour and their punishments follow:

Ex.22:
17 – You shall not allow a sorceress to live.
19 – Anyone who has intercourse with an animal must die. Anyone who sacrifices to other gods shall come under the ban.
25 – If you take another's cloak in pledge, you must return it before sunset.
27 – You shall not revile God nor curse a ruler of your people.

Ex.23:
1 – You must not make false assertions. Do not support the guilty by giving malicious evidence.
6 – You must not cheat any poor man of yours of his rights at law.
9 – You must not oppress the stranger….. you have lived as strangers in the land of Egypt.

Lev.15:
1-18 – Bodily discharges will render a man/woman unclean until evening, also anyone in contact with them.

Lev.18:
1-30 – Many sins in sexual relationships.

Lev.19:
20 – Sexual relationships with prohibited classes – slaves, concubines, a neighbour's wife…..

Lev.20:
10-27 – Death for sin in prohibited sexual relationships.

Numb.35:
16-30 – Death for murder or inconsiderate acts.

Deut.22:
13-28 – Serious punishments for sexual sins.

Deut,27:
15-26 – Curses and punishments for various sins.

Looking briefly at these texts, one cannot but be assured that the ancient Jews were so very much like ourselves, with our personal and community troubles. In order to maintain the conviction that the writer(s) of the Torah were worried about the *laissez-faire* attitude of the chosen people, the very people with whom Almighty God had made a covenant, and who were now proving themselves unworthy, both of the covenant and of the God who had brought them out of the slavery of Egypt, the ancient writers now had to consider the righteousness of the situation. If they were not worried, they would not have collected so carefully all the private and public sins enumerated in the books quoted above.

How therefore were they to prove to the people that the sins to which they had become accustomed – sins of lust, homosexuality, avarice, injustice, etc. – had become abhorrent to the eyes of the Almighty, that a severe punishment would await those who committed them? They therefore set themselves to teach the crowds of sinners that God is just, that they were to follow and listen to his admonitions; otherwise they would be liable to punishments befitting their crimes. They turned to the didactic method, being instructive, moralistic, and entertaining. The creation of the world, of man and woman, is the first of these attempts to teach God's creativity and generosity, as well as man's tendency to sin, particularly to unnatural sin, to which the early Jews were obviously so attached. The Catholic Church accepts the accounts of the Creation of the world, the First Sin and its inevitable consequences and punishment as ***divinely inspired***, not as a literal relation of historical events, but nevertheless important for the moral training of all mankind.

Gen.1:1 – 2:4 – [*Priestly version*] God created the physical world and the cosmos in six days. He saw that it was very good, and he rested on the seventh day.

Observations:

(1) No one was there to observe the gradual creative process – but modern scientific theories of evolution have much in their favour. The Didactic method – taken from a viewpoint of faith - shows that creation was brought about by the pure Will of God, and that the beauties of nature and of all creation come from his wisdom, his generosity, and his care to make all things work together, to make the world liveable. The Didactic Teacher (D.T.) explains to a rural society that creation must be loved and respected, coming as it is from the hand of God.

(2) He then shows that the tiller of the field and the farmer must observe rest on the seventh day, as God did. This became traditional in Jewish society, as in **Ex.20:8-11**; **Lev.23:32**; **Dt.5:12-15**, etc. – the Sabbath.

Gen.2:1- 3:24 – [*Yahvistic version*]. God creates man (**2:7**), to care for creation. He may eat of the fruit of any of the trees there, except those of the tree of good and evil, with punishment by death if he does, (**2:16-17**). God puts man in charge of all created beasts, to which he gives names (**2:18-21**). He then creates woman from one of man's ribs, to be his helpmate (**2:21-22**), and wife (**2:23-24**), and their nakedness did not shame them (**2:25**).

Observations:

(1) The D.T. shows that man is the master of creation; he can dominate it, but must care for it, under pain of death if he eats of this mysterious fruit of the tree of good and evil.

(2) The D.T. also shows that normal human sexuality is a good thing. The man evidently joins himself normally and sexually to his wife, (they become one body – **2:24b**), and their innocence avoids any shame due to their nakedness. There was no reason to be ashamed. (Moralistic teaching of the D.T., who was also interested in showing that <u>procreative sex</u> by the union of man and woman, to fill the earth (**1:28**), formed part of the plan of God. (This implies that ***any other form of non-procreative sex would not form part of the divine plan***).

(3) There were no fathers and mothers for the man to leave (**2:24a**). (Another moralistic teaching of the D.T., to be passed on and kept by future generations of the Jewish people, that procreative sex to give birth to offspring would be guaranteed by the fidelity of the spouses, having left their parental homes).

-o-o-o-o-o-o-o-

Enter the snake!

In mythology, the serpent symbolises fertility and procreation, wisdom, death, and resurrection (due to the shedding of its skin, which is akin to rebirth), and in the earliest schools of mysticism, the symbol of 'The Word' was the serpent. The 'light' that appeared was metaphorically defined as a serpent called 'Kundalini', coiled at the base of the spine to remain dormant in an un-awakened person. Divinity or awakening one's Godhood and latent abilities came with the rituals and teachings brought by the serpent people.

To understand them, we must look at the original 'serpents'. <u>In China</u>, it was a male and female pair with human heads and serpent bodies named Fu Xi and Nu Wa who created humans. <u>In Sumer</u>, it was the Annunaki Nin-Khursag and her husband Enki who were given the task of creating workers. Enki is known to us as the serpent in

Genesis—the one who gave us the ability to think and reason and so was cursed by his brother Enlil for it.

To the Hindus, it was the cosmic serpent Ananta who created us. So, if at the dawn of man's creation, we have a pair of serpent-like beings who created us, then those of the serpent cult must have been their direct descendants, either by blood or by spirit.

Serpents and snakes play a role in many of the world's myths and legends. Sometimes these mythic beasts appear as ordinary snakes. At other times, they take on magical or monstrous forms. Serpents and snakes have long been associated with good as well as with evil, representing both life and death, creation and destruction.

Serpents and Snakes as Symbols. In religion, mythology, and literature, serpents and snakes often stand for fertility or a creative life force—partly because the creatures can be seen as symbols of the male sex organ. They have also been associated with water and earth because many kinds of snakes live in the water or in holes in the ground. The ancient Chinese connected serpents with life-giving rain. Traditional beliefs in Australia, India, North America, and Africa have linked snakes with rainbows, which in turn are often related to rain and fertility.

As snakes grow, many of them shed their skin at various times, revealing a shiny new skin underneath. For this reason, snakes have become symbols of rebirth, transformation, **immortality,** and healing. The ancient Greeks considered snakes sacred to Asclepius, the god of medicine. He carried a caduceus, a staff with one or two serpents wrapped around it, which has become the symbol of modern physicians.

For both the Greeks and the Egyptians, the snake represented eternity. Ouroboros, the Greek symbol of eternity, consisted of a snake curled *into a circle or hoop, biting its own tail. The Ouroboros grew out of the belief that serpents eat themselves and are reborn from themselves in an endless cycle of destruction and creation.*

<u>In West Africa</u> the word Mossi is applied to a large group of peoples who inhabit the region on the southern side of the great bend of the river Niger. The anthropologist Mangin mentions the serpent as one of several animals which are kept in sacred groves in this region. Within the enclosure the animals, which include the crocodile and the leopard, are respected, but they may be killed if away from the sacred grove. The python is in some localities regarded as the guardian of the village. The reptile contains a guardian spirit which will accompany a traveller on his journey if asked to do so. It is forbidden to cut down or even to gather wood in the sacred grove. Every attempt is made to prevent a stranger from violating the sacred wood, but if restraint is impossible, the people will offer a sacrifice on his departure.

-o-o-o-o-o-o-o-

From consideration of the importance of the serpent in many ancient cultures, it seems clear that the ancient Jews also had some idea of this importance, and chose the snake symbol as a Didactic channel to show, from the time of the first created beings, that <u>sexual intimacy between man and wife, with the aim of procreation of children, is God's plan, and that anything outside of that plan is a disturbance of the divine order.</u>

Choosing the snake as symbol is of capital importance, as it symbolises the male sex organ, as mentioned above. Therefore, inasmuch as the "first parents" had already, one can reasonably and conveniently assume, used their God-given sexuality, just why was the snake chosen to invite the wife of the man to eat of the "forbidden fruit"? Given that they were not ashamed by their nakedness, it can be assumed that the snake's purpose was not to teach them how to use their sexuality, but <u>how to use it differently, in a different way, and for different purposes</u>.

The word "fruit" in the biblical story is "*poma*" from the Latin Vulgate. This has become "*pomme*" in French, and finally "apple" in English, giving rise to the traditional and mistaken idea that an apple was in fact the forbidden fruit. Because of its beauty, its delicious taste and texture, the fruit was used by the serpent to tempt the woman, whose curiosity was piqued by its offer of beautiful fruit. Joined to this admiration was woman's natural curiosity (known to the ancient D.T.!) to learn more, to improve her knowledge, to become by her acceptance "like God, knowing good and evil" (**Gen.3:6**).

The traditional curiosity of women was used by the D.T. to explain just why the woman accepted the serpent's invitation, and also explains just why, as men were habitually known (also known to the D.T.!) to follow the whims and fancies of their wives, the man in the story also ate of the "fruit" (**Gen.3:7**). *[This does not speak well of his ability to think for himself!].* Their eyes were opened, they realised that they were naked. So, they sewed fig leaves together to make loincloths [to cover their organs] (**Gen.3:7**). (D.T.: Thus was lost the original innocence of our first parents……).

Questions:

(1) <u>Why did the D.T. choose a serpent</u> to tempt the woman? Were there not other animals around?
Ans: Due to its strange mode of its life and its uncanny ability to move, feed itself, and procreate, the serpent had always been an enigma to ancient peoples. It was the most subtle of all the beasts that God had made (**Gen.3:1**), superior to all the four-legged

land creatures and the finned ones of the water, the perfect one therefore to be portrayed as the Tempter.

(2) <u>What was the snake's method of tempting the woman?</u>

Ans: There was no violence at all; its approach was insidious; its smooth-talking manner won the day. It preyed on woman's tendency to try novelties (in D.T.'s experience!), her weakness to doubt the word of God **(Gen.3:4-5)**, her ambition to be god-like, to know good and evil, to try new experiences, and her curiosity to eat the "fruit", which she did **(Gen.3:6)**.

(3) <u>What in fact could have been the "fruit"</u> that the woman, and her husband, who was with her, ate (**Gen.3:7**)?

Ans:
(a) The man was just as guilty as his wife – <u>he was there during the conversation</u> with the serpent, but said nothing at all to protest (Gen.**3:6b**). It was therefore a <u>joint sin of disobedience</u>, of insulting divine wisdom, of ruining God's plan for them. His guilt was as great as hers; they had jointly decided freely to try something new to them, which was within their power to attempt. This temptation had to be a pleasurable experience for them, or they wouldn't have tried it.

(b) The "fruit" depended on what the "first parents" considered to be "pleasure". For them, in a world of innocence, this meant the beauty of nature, the trees, the rivers, the animals, the climate, etc. etc. But there was one pleasure which surpassed all, which went far beyond the passing ones of enjoying the climate and the beautiful scenes provided by nature's surroundings. It was the pleasure of procreative sex together, providing joys far beyond those of nature, climate or anything else, filling their bodies and hearts with extreme sensations.

(c) <u>The "fruit" could have been only one thing</u>. The serpent had read correctly into their weakness, and used it to full advantage. If procreative sex had such an influence over them, why should they be constrained to use only procreative sex for pleasure? <u>Procreative sex had limitations</u>; every session together could produce offspring, that was clear. But other possibilities exist, and it would be up to them to find them.

<u>The temptation of the serpent to Adam and Eve</u> - How about trying <u>other ways of enjoyment</u>, ways that evidently exist in the physical capacity of both of you? These ways would <u>be non-procreative</u>, but would most certainly fulfil the enjoyment of sexuality! Endless enjoyment without consequences, that's for sure!

(d) And so, they ate the "forbidden fruit", a clear denial of God's instruction to them to "multiply and fill the world" (**<u>Gen.1:28</u>**). ***<u>Non-procreative sex could supply the same intense enjoyment as procreative sex, but would not have the same eventual effect, no worrisome offspring would be produced</u>***.

<u>For the D.T.</u>, it was evident that the unnatural sexual activities of the Jewish people, recently arrived from slavery, were a denial of God's plan. There would consequently be severe punishment. Childbearing would bring pain to womankind (**<u>Gen.3:16</u>**), hard work would be necessary for survival (**<u>Gen.3:19</u>**), death would come to all (**<u>Gen.3:19c</u>**), mankind would be banished from the happiness and innocence of Eden (**<u>Gen.3:23-24</u>**).

The D.T. saw that unnatural sex should be seen as the ultimate reason for the hardships and suffering of the Jewish people. For the D.T., ***<u>non-procreative intercourse in any form would be condemnable</u>***, whether practised by man or woman, and so these practices were condemned in the books of the Torah. They are also condemned to this day by the Catholic Church, seeing in them a continuation of the eating of the "forbidden fruit". [Encyclical ***Humanae Vitae*** 7/1968, of Pope St. Paul Vl (See Chap.20 – The Catholic Family)]

The Church has declared the Genesis account to be dogmatic, considering from the earliest centuries that Genesis is of divine inspiration. From this have come her teachings on Original Sin, the very first promise of a Redeemer and the need for redemption, joined to the eventual destruction of evil, symbolised by the serpent, and the role of the mother of the Redeemer as the Woman of the Book of Revelation. (See Chap17 – Feminine Element)

In today's modern culture, the texts of the Torah may seem very old-fashioned and outmoded, but there is clearly a strong affinity between them and the behaviour of many moderns, against which the Catholic Church and most of the manifold denominations of the Separated Brethren try to protest and correct, without great success, it must be admitted. Sexual predation abounds nowadays, there are movements ahead to allow sex with children, the medias are full of the adventures of people of high repute who have indulged in nefarious activities, whose pictures and stories are published worldwide. All this has certainly influenced the Catholic Church, giving her the publicity which she certainly did not desire, and has led to a diminishing of the moral content of the so-called eternal values which heretofore had formed part of Western Civilisation.

Perhaps it's now the moment for the modern world to take a look again at the ancient biblical didacticism once more, it could teach us a thing or two.

-o-o-o-o-o-o-o-

<u>Some more didactic texts in the OT.</u> In these texts <u>no third party was present</u> to record them, just one person and YHWH.

Gen.12:1-17; 27 – The effort of the post-exilic Jewish teachers to authenticate and justify their vocation of being Chosen.

Ex.3:1-18; 27 – The absolute certainty that man-made gods are inferior to YHWH, the One who chooses Moses and protects him during the 40-year desert sojourn. The ancient Jews may have been influenced by the elitist monotheism of the upper classes of Egypt, which certainly existed.

Ex.20; Dt.5: There are loose associations between the 10 Commandments and the Code of Hammurabi and the Nesilim (Code of the Hittite people), but the former is unique re the Sabbath and other prescriptions. Clearly a mixture of cultures!

Leviticus & Numbers – extremely long instructions by YHWH to Moses. Installation of laws and sacrificial rites. The Jewish leaders are justifying their presence and instructing the people, basing their teachings on the will of YHWH.

Judith 9: - Her very long prayer – effort by the Jewish leaders to show power of YHWH through a woman's prayer.

Esther 4:1-19 – A woman's prayer is superior to that of a man, Mordecai (**Est.4:8-17**).

Job 1- 42 – A meditation on God's goodness and his generosity to his faithful people.

Psalms 1-150 – Meditations on confidence in great distress. God will save, he is all-powerful.

-o-o-o-o-o-o-o-

<u>Two didactic texts in the NT</u>. No third party being present to record the event.

Mt.4:1-11 – Jesus tempted in the desert. The Evangelist gives an example how the believer must behave in front of temptations of luxury, pride, and power. The believer can overcome, just as Jesus did.

Lk.4:1- 13 – Jesus tempted by Satan in the desert. The same intention of the other Evangelist (above) is shown here, to encourage the believer to faithfulness and courage in the face of temptation. Satan never wins, if one is faithful!

-o-o-o-o-o-o-o-

O God, you are my God, for you I long;
For you my soul is thirsting.
My body pines for you
Like a dry, weary land without water.
So I gaze on you in the sanctuary,
To see your strength and your glory.
So I will bless you all my life
In your name I will lift up my hands.

(Ps. 62 (63), vs. 1-2, 4)

-o-o-o-o-o-o-o-

CHAPTER 8
Transubstantiation

Transubstantiation? Or Trans-substantiation?

Depending on how one pronounces the word, it's either with or without the hyphen. I've seen both renderings, so I'm not bothered. The Catholic Church prefers the first, but it really doesn't matter. What really matters is the importance that those who use either spelling give to the word. What exactly is meant by this curious word?

It is the word which has by itself divided many thousands of groups of believers in Jesus Christ from one another. It concerns the different interpretations that some believers give to the bread and wine used in their services. Some claim that the bread is changed into the very Body of Jesus, the wine into His Blood, while others maintain that the bread and wine are not changed at all, but remain merely symbols of His presence among mankind. Needless to say, this controversy has alienated many peoples, nations, and families from one another.

In "modern" times, the controversy began in the reign of Edward Vl, son of Henry Vlll of England, which had been a Catholic country from very early times. Here are the main sources of division which have occurred in that country.

In 1521, a decade before the break with Rome, King Henry Vlll published his book *"**Defence of the Seven Sacraments**", to defend Catholic doctrine against Martin Luther. Pope Leo X, to whom the book had been dedicated, rewarded him with the title of Defender of the Faith. Following Henry's break with Rome (1530), this title was revoked by Pope Paul lll in 1538, but was re-claimed by Parliament for the monarch in 1544. Under the Protectorate of the Cromwells (1653-59), it was not used, but was later bestowed on British monarchs by Parliament in 1707, and it is still held by them. Under Henry's son, Edward VI (1537-1553), the Church of England began to accept some aspects of European Protestant theology and rejected transubstantiation. Elizabeth I, as part of the Elizabethan Religious Settlement, gave royal assent to the Thirty-Nine Articles of Religion, which sought to distinguish Anglican from Catholic Church doctrine. The Articles declared that *"Transubstantiation (or the change of the substance of Bread and Wine) in the Supper of the Lord, cannot be proved by holy Writ; but is repugnant to the plain words of Scripture, overthroweth the nature of a Sacrament, and hath given occasion to many superstitions."*

Under the Test Act of 1673 [which excluded from public office (both military and civil) all those who refused to take the oaths of allegiance and supremacy, who refused to receive Communion according to the rites of the Church of England, or who refused to renounce belief in the Catholic doctrine of transubstantiation], Archbishop John Tillotson decried the *"real barbarousness of this Sacrament and Rite of our Religion", considering it a great impiety to believe that people who attend Holy Communion "verily eat and drink the natural flesh and blood of Christ. And what can any man do more unworthily towards a Friend? How can he possibly use him more barbarously, than to feast upon his living flesh and blood?"* (Discourse against Transubstantiation, London 1684, 35*).*

Anglicans generally consider no teaching to be binding that, according to the Articles, **"*cannot be found in Holy Scripture or proved thereby",*** but are not unanimous in the interpretation of such passages as **Jn.6,** and **1Cor.11**. Consequently, some Anglicans (especially Anglo-Catholics and some other High Church Anglicans) accept transubstantiation, while most Anglicans do not. In any case, nowadays even Church of England clergy are required to assent only that the Thirty-nine Articles have borne witness to the Christian faith. There is evident confusion here in these different points of view.

Official writings of the churches of the present Anglican Communion have consistently upheld belief in the Real Presence, a term that includes transubstantiation as well as several other eucharistic theologies such as consubstantiation, and the purely spiritual presence affirmed by the Thirty Nine Articles. Today, theological dialogue with the Catholic Church has produced common documents that speak of "substantial agreement" about the doctrine of the Eucharist.

What really is meant by this word, cause of such great controversy? Also, what does "substance" mean? Real Presence? Eucharist? Spiritual presence? Mass? Sacrament? The following pages are intended to clarify these different terms.

The background.

[The 16th century's problems really began with those of the late 14th and 15th centuries. The Turco-Mongol Muslim conqueror

Tamerlane (1336-1405) destroyed much of Asian and Indian cultures, capturing Moscow and much of Russia briefly; Islam captured **Constantinople** in 1453, to the horror of Western Europe, and the **Printing Press** was perfected by Gutenberg in 1455. The great discoveries of **Vasco da Gama, Magellan** and **Columbus** changed the politics of the world from the 1480s to the early 1500s. The disputed papacy of the Borgia family, **Pope Alexander VI** – who was able to unite Rome by the submissions of Ravenna, Naples and Milan through his son Cesare's military incursions, also avoided a war between Spain and Portugal in South America with the "Pope's Line", even though his life was unfitting to a Pope. The Catholic Church had been sorely affected by the effects of the **Black Death** of the 14th century, right into the 15th century. Many priests and Bishops had died, the remaining Bishops had several dioceses under their charge; nepotism and corruption had resulted and become endemic. Then came **Martin Luther**, a student of law who had become an Augustinian priest, (whose profiling and motivations for the priesthood would eliminate him from any such vocation in today's world). There were no Seminaries for training priests before the **Council of Trent** (1546-1563); before that one had to join a monastery or be apprenticed to a resident priest to be trained. These possibilities were completely changed under Trent, which decreed, among other decisions, the setting-up of seminaries in the Catholic nations of the time and the necessary courses to be followed]

Today's World.

Given that "Christianity" with its plethora of multiple differences of beliefs has been terribly divided since the 16th Century, when the efforts of the foremost original "Reformers" – Luther, Melanchthon, Zwingli, Bucer, Calvin, Knox, Henry Vlll – have blossomed into hundreds, indeed thousands (!) of non-Catholic "Christian" churches, one finds the following estimate:

The Center for Global Christianity of the Gordon-Conwell Theological Seminary, which is evangelical Protestant, <u>estimates</u> that there are currently **47,000** denominations to be found, worldwide, in 2018.

N.B.B. - "Christianity" above is decorated with inverted commas, since without these the common understanding would risk being that all Christians have the same beliefs, which is patently untrue. The same would apply to "Christian churches", as these are not only apparently and hopelessly divided, but many do not even profess the divinity of our Lord Jesus Christ, nor accept the Sacramental System, the role of the Virgin Mary, the saints, etc. etc.

<u>So, what really is the official teaching of the Catholic Church on this unusual word, this controversial subject?</u>

Transubstantiation is the Catholic teaching that at every Mass, at the consecration of the bread and the wine, they are *transubstantiated* (<u>4th Council of Lateran, 1215, preceded by Hildebert de Lavardin</u>, Archbishop of Tours (died 1133)), into the *sacramental* body and blood of Christ.

Several Church Fathers are cited by the Church to support its claim that the early Church embraced *transubstantiation* – St. Ignatius of Antioch(+107AD), Justin Martyr (+150AD), St. Irenaeus (+200AD), Tertullian (+200AD), St. Origen (+254AD), St. Ambrose of Milan (+397), St. Augustine (+430AD), etc. Now and then one or the other may have used the word ***symbol*** in the course of their deliberations, but that is only secondary to the main decision of transubstantiation held by these Fathers.

[Commenting on the *Test Act of 1673*, (cf.p.66, above) Archbishop Tillotson is completely erroneous in referring to the consecrated bread as the *"natural flesh and blood of Christ"*, as a *"feast upon his living flesh and blood"*. This has never been the teaching of the Catholic Church, which speaks of *"sacramental Body and Blood of Christ"*. **It is evident that the good bishop knew nothing of metaphysical thinking in philosophy.** His opinion has unfortunately been followed by the many thousands of inter-denominational "churches", which in the majority have no idea of the philosophical and metaphysical reasoning of the Catholic Church, not to mention its theology, for her teaching and belief].

In 1551, the Council of Trent confirmed the **Doctrine of Transubstantiation** as Catholic dogma, stating that *"by the consecration of the bread and wine there takes place a change of the whole substance of the bread into the substance of the Body of Christ our Lord, and of the whole substance of the wine into the substance of his Blood. This change the holy Catholic Church has fittingly and properly called transubstantiation"*.

Certain terms must also the brought in here,
so as to avoid any misunderstandings.

The first is **Consubstantial**, concerning the Holy Trinity. This was defined as an Article of Faith by many Councils, among them the 3rd Council of Constantinople (680 AD), 4th Lateran (1215 AD), General Council of Florence (1431 AD), and Vatican ll (1962). The 3rd of Constantinople defined against the heresy of the Cathars (aka Albigensians): *"The Father is from no one, the Son from the Father only, and the Holy Spirit equally from both"*. *The three are of the same substance (consubstantiales), fully equal, equally Almighty, equally eternal.* (See Chap.5 – The Incarnation)

The second is **consubstantiation**, concerning the Eucharist. This was a heresy, condemned by the Councils of Constance (1418 AD), Trent (1551 AD), and by Councils of Rome in the eleventh century. This theory claimed that the substance of Christ's Body exists together with the substance of the bread, and likewise the substance of His Blood exists with the substance of the wine. Basically, it denied the **Real Presence of Christ in the Eucharist.**

Some theologians have recently tried to explain what takes place at the Consecration, using the words: **Transignification** and **Transfiguration.** These words are unacceptable, because they do not specifically define the actual change of the substance of the bread and that of the wine being changed completely into the Body and Blood of Christ.

As Pope St Paul Vl wrote in *"Mysterium Fidei"* (1965) - ..."[these opinions]... *disturb the faithful and fill their minds with no little confusion about matters of faith. It is as if everyone were permitted to consign to oblivion doctrine already defined by the Church, or else to interpret it in such a way as to weaken the genuine meaning of the words or the recognised force of the concepts involved"*. *"Dominicae Cenae* (1980) of Pope St John-Paul ll clarifies this, saying *"If separated from its distinctive sacrificial and sacramental nature, the Eucharistic Mystery simply ceases to be".*

To be precise:

Q: What precisely are meant by ***"substance", "appearance",*** and ***"change"*** in the declaration of the Council of Trent?

The Gospel of St. **Jn.6**, provides the texts from which this doctrine and its refusals originate.

Jn. 6:51 *"I am the living bread, descended from heaven. He who eats of this bread will live forever. And the bread that I will give is my flesh for the life of the world".*

Jn. 6:55-56 *"My flesh is really food, and my blood really drink. He who eats my flesh and drinks my blood lives in me, and I in him".*

Although the Apostles believed in Him (**Jn.6:67-69**), many listeners went away, scandalised that he would want them to eat his body and drink his blood. The very idea of cannibalism, apart from its being prohibited by Jewish law, was totally abhorrent to them [and would be to us of today's thinking and laws]. Off they went, and no longer went about with him (**Jn.6:66**). He did not call them back to explain, nor to say that it was merely symbolic language, or sign language. He let them go, and capped this at the Last Supper when he instituted the Eucharist, proclaiming over bread and wine, *"Take and eat, for this is my Body…Take and drink, for this is my Blood"* (**Mt.26:26-28; Mk.14:22-24; Lk.22:19-20; 1Cor.11:24-25**), and *"Do this in memory of me"* (**Lk.22:19; 1Cor.11:25-26**)

Let us be clear and precise. This is no ordinary human being speaking. This is the very **Son of God, Second Person of the Most Holy Trinity.** Jesus claimed to be God Himself (**Jn.8:24b,58; 10:24-25,30**), Son of the Father (**Lk.22:70; Jn.19:7**), "One with the Father" (**Jn.10:30,38d;14:11;17:21**); to be the "Bread of Life" (**Jn.6:35,48,51**), "Light of the world" (**Jn.8:12**),"the Way, Truth and Life" (**Jn.14:6**), the "Good Shepherd" (**Jn.10:11,14**), the "Gate for the sheep" (**Jn.10:7,9**), the "True Vine"(**Jn.15:1**), the "Resurrection" (**Jn.11:25**). Spoken by this unique Person, his words must be taken very seriously. As the Bible-reading non-Christian Mahatma Gandhi did observe, *"This man was either crazy, or he was God".*

In Burkina Faso, a *"tribal ceremony of meal and drink to honour our ancestors"*, which I myself observed, is but an all-too-human effort to honour and recall their deceased forebears. Whereas the **Mass** (a word taken from the ancient sending-off of the faithful *"Ite Missa est"* – *"Go, you are sent forth"*) - celebrated daily in Catholic churches worldwide – is born of the assurance that the **Eucharist** ["thanksgiving"] is the very Body and Blood of Our Lord.

He himself had taught, that *"If you do not eat of the flesh of the Son of Man* [Dan.7:13-14], *and drink his blood, you will not have life in you* (Jn.6:53), *for my flesh is truly food, my blood is truly drink* (Jn.6:55). *The one who eats my flesh and drinks my blood has eternal life, and I will raise him up on the last day"* (Jn.6:54).

The Catholic Church teaches that the Eucharist is the **Real Presence** of Jesus among us. It is clearly therefore not a mere symbol, as others claim. The Mass therefore is not just a memorial for deceased forebears, as in the African tribe, it is a thanksgiving to the living Christ who gives his very Self to us. It is not merely a Spiritual Presence. The Mass does not look to the past, to the ancestors, but to the future and the fulfilment of the Lord's promise to raise those who partake of the Body and Blood offered to those who believe and accept.

But, just as many of His disciples went away and walked no more with him, scandalised at his words (**Jn.6:66**), in the same way many of the Separated Brethren unfortunately have done the same, just walking away because of their doubt and scepticism on hearing His words. (See Chap. 3 – The WORD).

"Substance" seems to have created heart-felt problems for many. It does not mean a merely physical and tangible thing one can observe and physically touch, there are other meanings. In ***meta*-physics** ["meta" meaning "change of the normal way of encountering reality"], *"substance"* [***substantia,*** in metaphysics] is to be understood as 'innermost reality', 'being', 'essence', 'essential reality', or 'nature' of a physical entity. ***"Reality"*** (also used as ***"substance"***) is <u>not</u> the tangible physical object, thing, or being in front of one, it is the definition of what that object/thing/being is <u>in itself</u>, its ***"essential nature"***. So, a dog is a dog is a dog, whether it be an Airedale, pit-bull, Pekingese, Alsatian, Chihuahua, or just plain mutt; its "dogginess" is inherent and essential to its <u>nature</u>, and so in any circumstances it will always be a dog. The same principle will also be applicable to any existent entity or being, animate or not. <u>The innateness – the inner specific uniqueness of the entity – is the reality – the substance - of its nature.</u>

It must be appreciated that, once an entity with its essential reality exists, absolutely no one can change that essential reality, except the One who had created its physicality. Therefore, <u>*no mere human can do this*</u>*.* **The Creator of the entity would be the only Person capable of doing so**, and this act would depend on His willingness to perform such an action.

<u>**"Appearances"**</u> or <u>**"Attributes"**</u> [also termed ***"accidents"*** in philosophy] are the physical, discernible, and/or tangible characteristics of a thing, being or object (i.e. its shape, composition, size, colour, weight, etc.). These may differ from being to being, (as for instance someone may be short, tall, squat, dark, pretty or not, male or female, all the while retaining the "person-ness" (humanity) of the individual in question). This principle is applicable to every existent entity of every individual species, so that the differences are of less importance, though the "appearances" may differ. Thus, a person will always be human, whether he/she is as yet unborn, a baby or aged person, pygmy,

Caucasian or Indo-Eurasian, intelligent or mentally-challenged, cab-driver or artist, notwithstanding the differences in appearance.

The Catholic Church therefore teaches that, <u>after</u> the Consecration at Mass, the ***"appearances"*** of bread and wine remain. That is, the bread and wine would <u>look</u> like bread and wine as before, would <u>taste</u> like bread or wine, would <u>weigh</u> the same and have the same colour, chemical composition, etc. BUT….

That which changes is the ***essential reality*** of the bread and wine, their ***"substance"***, so that they are no longer bread and wine in their "essential reality", but have in fact become the Body and Blood of the Lord, i.e. they have become <u>His</u> essential reality. There has been a **"substantial" change**, meaning a change in their very <u>nature</u>, and this has been brought about by ***the <u>creative word of Jesus Himself</u>, Second Person of the Trinity***. From its start the Church has continued to obey His command, in His Name (See ***"Do this in memory of me"***<u>: **Lk.22:19**</u>; <u>**1Cor.11:25-26.**</u>) – in <u>Chap.4 – The Covenants,</u>).

This is the reason why the Church teaches of the **Real Presence** of the Lord in the **Eucharist**, why she adores the Lord in the Eucharist at Benediction and in visits to the Blessed Sacrament, why people bend the knee on entering a church or chapel, and why it is so important to prepare oneself well to receive the Eucharist at Mass.

And it is also why there is often so much misunderstanding between Catholics and their Separated Brothers and Sisters. The former Anglican Archbishop of Canterbury Dr. George Carey once suggested "Eucharistic Hospitality", i.e. that the Catholic Church should allow sharing of the Eucharist as a means of fomenting unity among divided Christians. This was refused by the Catholic Church, as this would surely be "putting the cart before the horse".

For the Catholic Church, participation in the Eucharist is the goal of unity already attained, and not merely the means to attain that unity. She cannot and will never compromise over what is the very *essence* of her existence and hope, in the partaking of which is firmly believed to be the very Body and Blood of the Risen Lord. The Eucharist will never be used or considered to be a tool to mend the vagaries of our mutually sad history.

Transubstantiation must be understood to be the transfer of the innate nature, of the substantial, essential reality, the essentiality of the Divinity, into the essentiality of the receiving entity, while the specific and perceptible attributes of the recipient entity remain as before.

Creation from nothing, an attribute of Almighty God.

The "Priestly" tradition of Genesis tells us: "In the beginning God created the heavens and the earth" **(Gen.1:1)**. Having created "Light", God **called** it "day", and darkness He **called** "night" **(Gen. 1: 3-5)**. On the second day He created the vault above the water below, **calling** it "heaven" **(Gen.1:7-8)**. Then God caused the waters under heaven to come together, and let the dry land appear. He **called** the dry land "earth", and the mass of waters "seas" **(Gen.1:9-10)**. There follows the creation of many types of vegetation, of a light in the sky to rule the day, and another for the night; the creation of living creatures, every kind of wild beast and cattle, and reptile **(Gen.1:11-25)**, and God saw that it was "good". Finally, He created "in the image of himself, male and female", to be "masters over all the created world, the fish, the birds, the cattle, all the wild beasts, and reptiles" (**Gen.1:26-31**). Then God rested from all the work that He had done (**Gen.2:1-4**).

It is to be assumed that when all the various things and creatures were created, God ***called*** them by their species and name, although Genesis does not use the word ***called*** in all instances. But it is clear that when God creates, He *knows* the objects of his creation intimately, knowing not only their physical importance and role in his creation, but even their very *nature*.

To each entity of creation there are also created the laws of its particular existence. Thus, each matter (any "body" - liquids, physical beings, earth, etc) has its own interior and peculiar structure, as have also the created immaterials (air, gas, electricity), or the "spirituals" (free will, thought, decision, choice, faith, unbelief, etc). Each of the laws belonging to whichever entity must be obeyed for it to remain in existence, otherwise it would not exist as a separate and autonomous entity.

Whichever form the created entity may have, and howsoever it may exist, all depends on the *subsisting will* of its Creator for it to continue to exist. Thus, an amoeba, a mosquito or an elephant all would have to obey the laws of its particular existence – the amoeba will continue its one-celled existence in polluted water or in human bodies, the mosquito will continue to pollinate plants or to give diseases, the elephant will roam, gather in herds, and will grow its tusks of ivory.

These laws of matter and instinct will never change, unless the Creator decides otherwise. Being their Creator and sustainer, it is highly improbable that they ever will, unless He ***re-creates*** them through a further act of His divine will.

The belief in **_Transubstantiation_** must include, following from the preceding, the fact that it **_is a form of re-creation_**. There have been many **_acts of re-creation_** performed by Our Lord during his public life, using his divine power to do so. His miracles of healing, his mastership over nature and materials, his lordship over the death of humans, all show that He is in fact using this power to overcome the terrible things which can happen to people. In each of these re-creative acts, He clearly acts upon **physical matter and on the substance** *["essential reality"]* of the entity involved. These acts of re-creativity cannot be separated from the two inherent characteristics of the said entity, its appearances *["attributes"]* and nature *["essential reality"]*, **both of which may be acted upon**, e.g. the wine at Cana, though at times only one is, e.g. the bread and wine at Mass remain with the same physical attributes, only their innate nature has been changed.

There are in fact many instances in the Gospels which show connections between creation and links or transfers of nature, of *substantiality*. Here are some of these:

1) The very first is the mystery of the Incarnation.

    From the moment that the Virgin Mary said **"Let it be done to me according to thy word"** (**Lk.1:38**), there has occurred a union of the *essential reality* of the *divinity* of the Second Person of the Trinity with the *essential reality* of the *humanity* of the ovum in Mary's womb. In other words, without any change whatsoever of the innate humanity of the ovum in her womb, there has been produced the mystery of *the unity of two different natures* (****Hypostatic Union**). Thus, Jesus the Person has two natures from the very moment of conception, which is one of the fundamental teachings of the Catholic Church, (**Council of Chalcedon, 451 AD**).

In the Incarnation, there is a *creative* joining of the *substantiality* of the divinity with the *substantiality* of the human. A real and true linking of two separate *essential realities* had taken place, each with its individuality, due to God's will. Mary had been chosen to bear the Son of the Father (**Lk.1:31-34, 35**). There has in fact occurred the creation of a completely unique being, Jesus Himself (***Athanasian Creed).

2) The wedding at Cana. (**Jn.2:1-12**). Here we see once again the transfer of *essential reality* of one entity into the *essential reality* of another. Through his divine power of Son of God, in order to avoid the family's embarrassment, and to obey his mother (!), Jesus has in fact exercised an act of re-creation, **which only the Creator could perform**. The *essential reality* of water has been changed into the *essential reality* of wine; the clarity (*attribute*) of water remains. The other attribute of water, *taste*, is also changed. There has in fact been a miracle of re-creation/transubstantiation performed by the Creator of both water and wine, in which the *essential reality* of water has been radically altered, an act of which only its Creator is capable, while its *attribute* (lack of colour) has remained. Jesus has acted both upon its physical reality (*taste*), as well as upon its *essential nature*.

N.B.- While all the Separated Brethren accept this biblical miracle as authentic, performed without a word but by simple will from the **WORD***, yet they still refuse to accept that which took place at the Last Supper, coming from the* **WORD** *himself, giving himself for the salvation of all, and see his words as merely symbolic. The fundamental illogicality of this long-held refusal makes the Saviour a teller of myths, a charlatan, a liar.* **He just couldn't have meant what he** *had said!* (Exactly what had happened when some had walked away (**Jn.6:66**)!)

3) The miracles of healing on humans – the lepers, (**Mt.8:1-4; Lk.17:11-19**); the blind – (**Mt.9:27-31; Mk.8:22-26**); the paralysed – (**Mk.2:1-12**); the possessed – (**Mk.9:14-29**), the deceased – (**Mk.5:35-43; Lk.7:11-17; Jn.11:41-44**), show the ***re-creative power*** of Jesus over [human] matter. In all these ministrations Jesus shows his capability to ***re-create*** the bodies of the disabled or the dead, bringing them once again to the <u>perfection intended</u> by God, showing a total mastery over both *matter* and its *essential reality*. ***Re-creation!***

He also shows his <u>mastery over [inanimate] matter</u>: the creation/multiplications of loaves and fishes: (**Mt.14:13-21; Lk.9:12-17**); the calming of the storm (**Mk.4:35-41**); the walking on water (**Mk.6:45-52**); his preparing of breakfast for his Apostles who had been fishing (**Jn.21:9-12**). Shining examples of ***re-creation!***

4) The Last Supper: - During this last meal, Jesus took bread and wine, and said to his disciples:

"Take and eat, for this is my Body...Take and drink, for this is my Blood" (**Mt.26:26-28; Mk.14:22-25; Lk.22:19-20; 1Cor.11:24-26**). These are two ***miracles of essential re-creative change*** that Our Lord performs.

When Our Lord had pronounced these impossible and mind-blowing words, we should not doubt that he meant every syllable. The bread and the wine of the repast have been in fact <u>transubstantiated</u> into His very Body and Blood, while retaining totally the <u>appearances</u> (*attributes*) of ordinary bread and wine. Once again, only the Creator of the matter [the bread and the wine] has the ability to change the *essential realities* of these simple entities into His very Body and Blood. He has in fact **re-created** them, changing the *natures* of ordinary bread and wine into the *divine natures* of His own Body and Blood. He has not changed their physical appearance, but has acted only upon their *essential nature.*

That has always been the firm belief of the Catholic Church, notwithstanding everything that normal human senses or mentality could oppose. This is indeed the tremendous mystery of **Transubstantiation, the re-creation of one essential reality into another,** celebrated at every Mass throughout the entire world. This began in Apostolic times (**Acts 2:47**), and will continue to the end of time (**Mt:28:20**). (See Chap.4 – The Covenants).

"Do this in memory of me" (**Lk.22:19; 1Cor.11:25-26**) – This refers to the essential ministry of His priests, who have thereby received both the command and the capacity to continue this rite of sacramental offering instituted by Jesus, always understood to have been the Sacrament of Orders, the Priesthood. (See Chap.4 – The Covenants)

-o-o-o-o-o-o-

Assertio Septem Sacramentorum (Defence of the Seven Sacraments, by Henry Vlll), which defended the sacramental nature of marriage, and the supremacy of the Pope.

Hypostatic Union - The "**hypostatic union**" is an important **theological concept** to understand about the person and work of Jesus Christ. It basically says that Jesus Christ is one Person, having two natures (divine and human). A normal human person is a hypostasis endowed with reason. Moreover, hypostasis and nature are related to each other in such a manner that the hypostasis is the bearer of the nature and the ultimate subject of all being and acting, while the nature is that through which the hypostasis exists and acts.

The Council of Chalcedon [451 AD] issued the Chalcedonian Definition, which repudiated the notion of a single nature in Christ, and declared that he has two natures in one Person and hypostasis. It also insisted on the completeness of his two natures: Godhead and manhood.

***The Athanasian Creed (St Athanasius +373AD), recognized this doctrine and affirmed its importance, stating that "He is God from the essence of the Father, begotten before time; and he is human from the essence of his mother, born in time; completely God, completely human, with a rational soul and human flesh; equal to the Father as regards divinity, less than the Father as regards humanity. Although he is God and human, yet Christ is not two, but one. He is one, however, not by his divinity being turned into flesh, but by God's taking humanity to himself. He is one, certainly not by the blending of his essence, but by the unity of his person. For just as one human is both rational soul and flesh, so too the one Christ is both God and human."

> On my bed I remember you,
> On you I muse through the night
> For you have been my help;
> In the shadow of your wings I rejoice.

My soul clings to you,
Your right hand holds me fast,
(Ps. 62(63), vs. 6-8)

-o-o-o-o-o-o-o-

CHAPTER 9
The Mass

So, what really is the Mass?

This question is not too far-fetched, as in the 50 years of my priesthood I have met few who could give a coherent answer to it. Most practicing Catholics go to church on Sunday, listen carefully to the readings, kneel, stand, respond, and sit at the appropriate times. They pray for themselves, for their families, or for someone else who has asked for prayers, receive Holy Communion, then leave, fully satisfied that their Sunday obligation has been fulfilled. Good for them, and long may this marvellous tradition continue.

But to the question above, many would say: "The Mass is a place of peace…of love…of community….of hearing the word of God… the place where I receive the Lord as He has asked me to do". These and similar replies are good, but they don't say what really the Mass - *is*!

10-year old Kizito in Burkina once replied to my question during the First-Communion preparation class with *"In the Mass, Jesus gives himself to me, so that I can give myself to him!"*. Marvellous – he's now become a priest! But still, not the answer to the question.

Apart from the usual personal ideas and replies, no God-fearing Catholic, in my experience, has ever clearly said what the Mass really is. Maybe because they haven't learnt, or perhaps because, as some would say, *"That's not my work, that's for the clergy to know!"* They may be right, so here is my attempt to give an answer, keeping to the near side of intelligibility.

In the first place, Jesus and his Apostles had to prepare for the Passover feast of their people, the Jews **(Mt.26:17-19**; **Mk.14:12-16; Lk.22:7-13)**. This was the Seder meal, where a real lamb had been sacrificed and eaten in the family, intended to recall the Passover of the Spirit of the Lord at the time of the liberation of the Jewish slaves from Egypt (**Ex.12:1-14**).

The great difference was that Jesus, the true Lamb of God (**Jn.1:30, 36**), consecrated bread and wine, declaring them to be his very Body and Blood, to be eaten and drank (**Mt.26:26-29; Mk.14:22-25**; **Lk.22:19-20; 1Cor.11:24-26**). From earliest times, the Church has always considered this Passover meal to have been the First Mass. This was to authenticate his words in **Jn.6:32-58** – the "Discourse on the Bread of Life". This shocked many, and so they stopped following him (**Jn.6:60, 64-66**), but the Apostles stayed, Peter saying *"Lord, to whom shall we go? You have the words of eternal life!"* (**Jn.6:67-69**).

When Jesus said to the Apostles **"Do this in memory of me",** he was in fact inaugurating the Sacrament of Orders, the priesthood to continue his work and message, and this had been understood as such from earliest times. The first Christian community remained faithful to the Apostles, and to the breaking of bread (**Acts 2:42,46**). Throughout all her history, the Church – called "Catholic" by St Ignatius of Antioch in 107 AD – founded by Jesus on Simon the Fisherman (**Mt.16:18-20**), has considered this special rite, started by Jesus himself, to be the most sacred of all her rituals, to be the *"source and summit of the Christian life"*. (Vatican ll **"Lumen Gentium"** No.11).

By the very words of consecration, the Mass is in itself a miracle; belief in the efficacity of the words used by Jesus, and by those appointed by the Church, is totally founded on the delegation pronounced by Our Saviour. In its present form, the Mass differs very little from its original form. The word "Mass" itself is taken from *"Ite Missa Est"* (*"Go, you are sent forth"*) at the end of the ceremony, taken from its former use of the Latin language.

The great difference between the Jewish Seder and the Catholic Mass is the fact that in the Seder a real lamb was sacrificed, whereas at Mass Our Lord, the real Lamb of God, offers himself as a sacrifice for mankind in *an unbloody manner*, using bread and wine.

(Be patient, dear reader, we're getting there!)

Let us consider the Mass to be somewhat like a beautiful cake. There are lovely decorations all around the cake, and these are in fact, in the Mass, the hymns with music, the readings, the homily, and the sending forth at the end. But...where does the "cake" come in?

After the homily and the Profession of Faith and Prayer of the Faithful, there is the Eucharistic Prayer, of which there are several examples. Each contains blessings, prayers for the sick and deceased, for particular persons, for the leaders of the Church, for Separated Brethren.......

But the most important part of the Eucharistic Prayer consists of a **re-actualisation** of the three most important events which took place in the life of Our Lord, of the Church, of all humanity. <u>These three events</u> are not a mere memorial, they <u>are a **celebration of the memorial**</u> of the Passion, Resurrection, and Ascension of Jesus, as specified in the Eucharistic Prayers. <u>They are a **re-actualisation of historic events**</u> which actually happened to Our Lord, and which are re-actualised by the presiding priest, according to the words of Jesus *"Do this in memory of me"*. (See <u>Chap.4 – The Covenants</u>)

The ***First event*** is that of the First Mass on Holy Thursday, when the priest uses the same words of Jesus *"This is my Body, take and eat"; "This is my Blood, take and drink"*. This is the same consecration as performed by Jesus.

The ***Second event*** is that of Good Friday, showing the death of Jesus by the two separate consecrations of bread and wine, showing the separation of his Body from his Blood, i.e. his Death.

The ***Third event*** is the Resurrection of Jesus on Easter Sunday. This is celebrated by the priest breaking off a small portion of the Body of Our Lord – the consecrated Bread - and dropping It into the Precious Blood in the chalice, showing that his Body and his Blood are now reunited. Jesus is really alive, in faith and in fact!

The final decoration on the cake is the reception of the Eucharist, which we do with care and love. After a suitable pause for a prayer of thanksgiving, we are sent out to "Love and serve the Lord". Final hymn and music. Amen.

When therefore people assist at Mass, at any Mass, <u>those present are in fact re-actualised</u> and are placed into the presence of Our Lord and his Apostles once more in the Cenacle. <u>They are in fact thrown back spiritually in time and space</u> into these three capital events, into the Cenacle at the First Mass, into Golgotha, and into the Holy Sepulchre, at the Resurrection. It is good to know that the presence of Our Lord at Mass, and in the Eucharist, are the greatest blessings possible. These are some of the most productive themes of a meditation, one can hardly be more present to Our Lord than in meditating on this tremendous theme.

The Mass should be taken seriously, the stages of the ceremony followed with care, Holy Communion received gratefully and with love, provided one is in a state of Grace. Personal resolutions should be taken to live according to the precepts of Our Lord. One can hardly imagine a greater blessing than to live in Christ, who gave himself for our eternal happiness.

Into Your hands, Lord!
In manus tuas, Domine!

All day long I hope in you,
Because of your goodness, Yahweh.
Remember your kindness, Yahweh,
Your love, that you showed long ago.
Do not remember the sins of my youth;
But rather, with your love, remember me.

(Ps. 24(25), vs. 5-7)

-o-o-o-o-o-o-o-

CHAPTER **10**

Resurrection Proof

Proof of Christ's Resurrection by the Shroud of Turin

Most people, whether or not too interested in the subject, have heard or read of the Shroud of Turin, which is, according to reliable scientific sources, is, and has been for a number of years, the most investigated ancient artifact ever known. This is too big a subject to go into here, but it is enough to know that every available discipline known to modern science has been brought to bear on this strip of linen cloth, believed to be the very cloth which had been used to wrap the body of Jesus after its removal from the Cross and its deposition in the tomb of Joseph of Arimathea (**Mt.27:57-61**). Science has decided conclusively that the Shroud reveals that a real person had been crucified. This burial cloth bears on itself the strange marks of a crucified body, marks which to this day mystifies science, but which correspond to the details of the torture and sufferings administered to and undergone by Jesus. The marks have no trace of paint, and it is not yet known just how, and by what method, they have been put there. Whole libraries have been filled with books concerning the Resurrection of Jesus, and this little paper maintains that the Shroud itself is absolute proof of this most debated, mysterious, and important subject. It is hoped that its careful reading may lead to further interest in the subject and belief in what should concern everyone, the possibility of eternal happiness, and the promise by Jesus that he will return in glory to "make all things new" (**Rev. 21:5**).

It is necessary to follow, step by step, the Gospel accounts of the death of Jesus, his burial, and what happened afterwards.

[A] – The Death of Jesus

> Mt.27:50 – Jesus, crying out with a loud voice, yielded up his spirit.
>
> Mk.15:37 – Jesus gave a loud cry and breathed his last
>
> Lk.23:46 – Jesus cried out in a loud voice *"Father, into your hands I commit my spirit"*. With these words, he breathed his last.
>
> Jn.19:30 – After Jesus had taken the vinegar, he said *"It is accomplished!"* And, bowing his head, he gave up his spirit.

[B] – The Burial of Jesus

> Mt.27:57-61 – Joseph took the body, wrapped it in a clean shroud, and put it in his own tomb, which he had hewn out of the rock.
>
> Mk.15:42-47 – [Pilate]…granted the corpse to Joseph, who bought a shroud, took Jesus down from the cross, wrapped him in the

> shroud, and laid him in a tomb which had been hewn out of the rock

> Lk.23:50-56 – [Joseph]…asked for the body of Jesus. He then took it down, wrapped it in a shroud, and put him in a tomb which was hewn in stone, in which no one had yet been laid.

> Jn.19:38-42 - [Pilate]…gave permission…they took the body of Jesus…wrapped it with the spices in linen cloths…. there was a garden… [with]…a new tomb in which no one had yet been buried…they laid Jesus there.

[C] – **1st Day** – **Friday**. Jesus died on this day, before sunset. It was also the Day of Preparation for the Sabbath (the Jewish day of rest – today's Saturday). [Roman] guards were placed by Pilate on the Jewish leaders' request, and seals were put on the stone (**Mt.27:62-66**).

Role of the guards. How many were on guard there?

> (1) Their number is unknown, but '*some*' went to tell "the priests all that had happened" (**Mt.28:11**) [If there had been only 2, one would have been mentioned as 1, (the other guard left would have been unwilling to remain by himself, for security's sake); if there had been 3, 'some' would implicitly refer to 2, leaving 1 behind at the tomb – this is probable, but again unlikely, for security's sake. Therefore, there must have been at least 4 guards].

These were hardened soldiers, signed on for 25 years of service [Roman army law], and not accustomed to slacken on duty. Most probably the 'beaters' at the scourging of Jesus (**Mt.27:26**;

Mk.15:15; **Jn.19:1**) were soldiers, Roman or barbarian, happy to be allowed to severely punish a helpless Jew.

(2) They were placed at the tomb to avoid any possibility of the body being stolen and Resurrection claimed afterwards (**Mt.27:62-66**).

Arguments against the possibility of the body being stolen.

(a) No practising Jew would have dared to steal the body, as

(b) Touching a dead body would incur defilement (e.g. – **Num.19:11**; **Lk.10.30-37**).

(c) Removing the body would be considered work, against the Law prohibiting work on the Sabbath, thus it would be contrary to Jewish obedience to the Law (**Ex.20:8-11**)

(d) No Roman would want to steal a dead Jew's body, of one who had been crucified by Pilate's decree. His life would have been forfeit!

Structure of the tomb.

(a) It had never contained anyone, being new, and hewn out of the rock (**Mt.27:60**; **Mk15:46**; **Lk.23:54**; **Jn.19:41**).

(b) A large [circular] stone was rolled against the entrance to the tomb (**Mk.15:47**); a stone had been rolled against the entrance (**Mt.28:3**).

(c) The spices and stone were part of the Jewish burial customs (**Mt.26:13**; **Lk.23:56**; **Jn.19:40**).

2ⁿᵈ Day – **Saturday** was the Sabbath – no work was to be done – it was not allowed (**Ex.31:12-17**).

3ʳᵈ Day – **Sunday** – towards dawn (**Mt.28:1**; **Mk.16:2**; **Lk.24:1**; **Jn.20:1**)

(a) An angel descended…rolled away the stone… the guards became like dead men (**Mt.28:4**). [The angel] …spoke to the women…sent them to tell the apostles Jesus had "risen from the dead" (**Mt.28:6-7**).

(b) The stone had been rolled back (i.e. circular in shape). They met a young man seated on the right-hand side (**Mk.16:5**). He told them Jesus was risen (**Mk.16:6-7**).

(c) Two men in brilliant clothes suddenly appeared (**Lk.24:5**), who said to them that "Jesus has risen" (**Lk.24:6-7**).

(d) Mary of Magdala saw that the stone had been "moved away from the tomb" (**Jn.20:1**)….Peter and "the other disciple" [John] came running, saw "the linen cloths on the ground…but the "head cloth rolled up in a place by itself" (**Jn.20:1-8**).

Further arguments against the possibility of body-theft.

(a) The exterior presence of at least 4 armed Roman soldier-guards.

(b) At least three men would have been necessary to remove the body. Based on the Shroud's measurements, Jesus would have weighed about 175 lbs.

(c) No man or men had approached the tomb, but the guards became like dead men [were stricken senseless] at an angel's appearance (**Mt.28:1-4**). Fear had struck them.

(d) The guards had been bribed (**Mt.28:11-15**) to say that the body had been stolen while they slept. (This is a poor reflection on the professionalism of the Roman army – could 4 guards not have been awakened by [supposedly] 3 men who (i) first would have had to get past them, (ii) roll the stone away (iii) lift up a heavy body, and (iv) get past the them again, without awakening them? ***This is ridiculous!***

(e) The whole scenario is ridiculous, reflecting on the naivete of the Jews who believed this cocktail of lies (**Mt.28:15**). This belief continues to this very day in 2020 AD.

(f) It says much for the cleverness of the Jewish leaders that they were able to trick the tough

Pilate into believing their lies, but not so much of his ability as Governor of Palestine.

[D]- Role of the Shroud of Turin.

The Shroud shows precise non-smudged blood marks, now identified as the rare type AB. The body must have been washed (*Zugibe, pages 218-227), as:

(a) The bodily wounds would have clotted shortly after death, and, being hardened, would not have left clear marks on the Shroud.

(b) After washing, the wounds would have oozed fresh blood again, thus being able to leave fresh marks on the Shroud.

(c) No removal of the body had been performed, as:

(i) no smudging of the blood-marks had occurred, and

(ii) no known method of imprinting the contours of the body could take place.

[E] – Conclusion – no handling of the body had taken place.

[F] – John's Gospel states that Jesus had passed through locked doors after the Resurrection (**Jn.20:19-20, 26-27**), and Luke says that he disappeared after "breaking the bread" at Emmaus (**Lk.24:30-32**). His body is now glorified, (i.e. under control of his will and spirit).

[G] – As in [F] above, Jesus had most probably passed through the Shroud's tissue at the moment of his Resurrection. He is now totally in control of his body's movements. The mere cloth of the Shroud could not retain him.

Q: (**Jn.20:21-23**): How did Jesus pass through doors, locked through fear of the Temple police (**Jn.7:32,45-47**)?

Ans: In passing through doors, he shows that his risen-glorified body is under the full control of his will and spirit. All matter is now subject to his will and spirit's control. Nothing, neither cloth, wood nor stone, can now retain him.

(See Chap.3 – The WORD).

[H] – Science cannot explain how the marks came to be imprinted upon the Shroud, even after multiple scientific tests (STURP – Shroud of Turin Research Project - the 1978 investigation on the Shroud in Turin, Italy).

[I] – **Final Conclusions**: It is clear that:

(a) The guards had been unable to prevent the Resurrection.

(b) To save face, the Jewish leaders had bribed them.

(c) No removal of the body by human hands had been performed, or was even possible, given the presence of the Roman guards at the entrance of the tomb.

(d) Peter and John had entered the tomb, and, having seen the [flattened-out] wrappings lying there, had believed in the Resurrection of Jesus.

(e) The Apostles most likely would have taken the Shroud with them to the company of the other Apostles, as proof of the Resurrection.

(f) It is the Shroud itself which is the only tangible object which had enrolled the tangible body of Jesus.

(g) The Shroud contains markings upon it, the cause of which is mysterious to this day. Given the meticulous series of tests and investigations carried out in Turin and elsewhere, it is therefore absolute proof of the Resurrection of Jesus.

(h) No person seems to have been involved in the production of these markings, whose cause is as yet totally unknown.

(i) No form of art or artist was involved, as the markings themselves are in negative form, any photo of which comes out as positive. No artist could ever have painted in negative form, nor could any artist have dreamed of such a possibility.

(j) Ergo, the S*hroud of Turin itself is absolute proof of the Resurrection of Jesus Christ.*

-o-o-o-o-o-o-o-

*Frederick T. Zugibe M.D. PhD.: **"The Crucifixion of Christ"**, ISBN 978-1-59077-070-2

-o-o-o-o-o-o-o-

See, my servant shall prosper,
He shall be lifted up, exalted,
Rise to great heights.
As the crowds were appalled on seeing him,

So disfigured did he look
That he seemed no longer human;
So will the crowds be astonished at him
And kings stand speechless before him;
For they shall see something never told,
And witness something never heard before.

(Is.52:13-15)

-o-o-o-o-o-o-o-

CHAPTER 11
The Trinity

Why *Trinity?*

Well, why? Why not Duality? Or just Unity? Or Multiplicity? Why any Deity at all? But, ***Trinity?*** Well….

For centuries people have been grappling with the problems of the existence, nature, personality, numerology, of God. Great philosophers, saints, atheists, agnostics, humanists, writers, humanitarians, of many nations and cultures, have wrestled with these problems, have come up with great certainties, possibilities, doubts, refusals.

Let me be clear about this. I do not subscribe to any of the positions of these great men. I'm just an octogenarian priest in a basement, mulling over the very same problems. But that does not mean that I have no right to opinions, no right to express them. So, at 82 plus years, I venture to state my views and opinions. Do bear with me……

I start by declaring that I do believe in the existence of a Personal God. My training and Faith have helped me to understand the proofs for him as Father [because Jesus had thus referred to him], of his existence. I have followed and accepted the proofs of Aquinas – those of the Unmoved Mover, the Uncaused Cause, the Contingency factor etc,- and those of other saints. All very well and good, but I now tend more to accept the <u>Illative Sense of John Henry Newman</u>, recently canonised, which, according to him, is "The power of judging about truth and error in concrete matters". This Sense is, according to him, analogous to the mathematical calculus of modern times. On this reasoning even in experimental science, truth can be found by application of the Illative Sense, which gives it its sanction.

So, just why do I believe in an Almighty and Personal God as Father? Simply because, based on the reasoning of the Illative Sense, the alternative would be utter absurdity, taking all the factors into consideration. The mathematical probabilities of the universe and the enormity of its most minute laws, of the atoms, protons, neutrons, of the Boson-Higgs particle, of germs and viruses, of the migratory phenomena of birds, turtles, antelopes, whales and fish, even of tiny butterflies, of this little planet to which we cling, of the regularity of its seasons, of its innumerable life-forms of flora and fauna, of it even existing, are so overwhelmingly improbable, that the application of the Illative Sense impedes me from denying the unlikeliness of why anything should exist at all. Ergo, where there is order on scales both so vast and so minute, there is necessarily a Supreme Intelligence, which I consider to be divine. Any Neanderthal would have come to the same conclusion, of course!

There is more. Having been nurtured in the Catholic-Christian tradition, I believe that this Supreme Intelligence – personified as Father by Jesus, is capable of emotion, particularly of Love, the greatest of all (**1Jn.4:8,16**), even greater than mere human love, and that this Divine Love has itself become human in His Son Jesus the Messiah, who fulfilled so completely the ancient prophecies of the Jewish faith (**Mt.5:17**). I believe in Jesus the Son of the Almighty Father. I share in his humanity, believe in his historical authenticity, in his incomparable teachings, nowhere else even imagined or proclaimed. I believe in the one visible Church he founded (**Mt.16:13-20**); in his rejection, condemnation and death on a Cross by Jewish and Roman complicity, in his return to actual life (See Chap.10 – Resurrection Proof). I believe that by shedding his Blood he has saved all human beings *in potentia*, and has promised eternal life to those who *"eat and drink of my Body and Blood"* (See Chap.9 – The Mass), and I believe that he will return, as Judge of both the living and the dead.

(See Chap.20 – The Catholic Family).

That being said, there is a third factor to consider, called Spirit. These Three, according to the majority of Christian groups (which excludes the Unitarians and several others), are the Holy Trinity. How to explain One is hard enough, but Three poses many other problems (!), but I strongly believe in the real existence and presence of the Holy Spirit in the world, from Creation (**Gen.1:2**), to Pentecost (**Acts 2:1-13**), when the Church is born among non-Jewish peoples, to Its role in instructing the Church through the centuries (**Jn.16:12-13**), using the Great Councils as channels of instruction, keeping the Church from falling into the ever-present danger of heresy (See Chap. 5 – The Incarnation).

Having shown the content of my faith in a Personal and Triune God, I ask, what do non-Christian religions hold as their major set of beliefs? The debate opens by briefly considering ancient and extant religions.

The ancient Greeks, Romans and Egyptians, all had many gods, each with a function similar to human activities – some were messengers, some dedicated to war, others to blacksmithing, others to love, beauty, intelligence, planting, reaping, etc. But there was no one Personal God to whom to relate, and these many gods were finally supplanted by the Christian message, their names now remembered by having been given to the planets, days of the week, months of the year.

Hinduism believes in one god, Brahman, the greatest of three, the two others being Vishnu and Shiva. "He" has 33 million "avatars" or characteristics which have names and personalities. These are not gods, but in paying obeisance to them, the Hindu can attain the presence of Brahman, but first he must pass through an indefinite series of Reincarnations in order to attain Nirvana, the blessed after-life, considered to be a form of natural happiness after death. It is only by **Moksha**, union with Brahman, that the Hindu can escape from the series of reincarnations, attested to by the Bhagavat Gita, one of the foremost Hindu scriptures.

On considering non-Christian Eastern groups, the Confucianism of China and Shinto of Japan are ancestor and humanist cults. These lean towards the establishment of enlightened humanistic societies, there is no Personal God either, as they lean towards mere humanity, without investigating the causes and ends of humanity. Greek philosophy is lacking - they need Plato and Aristotle!

The belief in an Indian prince called Gautama, who had seen the "Light" and who had become Buddha, the "Enlightened One", and who had decided to spread it, has become the Buddhist faith of several far-Eastern countries – Korea, Thailand, Myanmar, China etc., and has even spread into several Western countries, many now even denying their Christian roots.

Buddhism is somewhat similar to Confucianism and Shinto, but according to St John-Paul ll in **Threshold of Hope** (1994), *"it is largely atheistic, i.e. the world is evil, and perfect liberation from it [the evil world] is to attain Nirvana (perfect indifference to the* *world's evil), thus there is no God possible".* The groups mentioned all believe in the series of reincarnations, escape from which can only come thru extinguishing the "three fires" – passion, aversion, ignorance – especially in Buddhism.

The above are quite contrary to the faith of Catholicism, which believes in one God, rejects rebirth, reincarnation, and Nirvana. One is born, is responsible for one's life, and will be judged at death for the manner of behaving while alive. The great problems of predestination and free will also come into the basic theological thinking of the Catholic Church.

How therefore to "explain" the seeming conundrum of the Trinity, seeing that other non-Christian groups also have valid arguments in favour of one Personal God? Judaism and Islam each have a Uni-Personal God, but while the former consider YHWH (Yahweh, now called Ha-Shem, the "name") as their own one God, and live calmly while still awaiting the Messiah and obeying the Law of Moses, the one God of Islam, Allah, is one of belligerence, not of love, whose adepts consider it their duty to convert the world to obedience to Allah, by violence if necessary. I do not therefore accept their Uni-Personal Gods under these conditions; the one whose prophecies in the Old Testament I believe have been completely fulfilled in Jesus the Christ, the other where individual choice of a faith is denied, among many other contradictory expectations.

Were the Personal God only a Unity, there would certainly arise the aberrations of behaviour clearly visible by the application of belief by his adepts, seen by the results given by Judaism (e.g. **Joshua 11:5-9**), and Islam (e.g**. Qur'an Sura 8:13-17**), through the many past centuries, to this very day.

In fact, many Jews of today have become largely agnostic, but are determined to hold on to their land at whatever cost, because of their belief that it was given in perpetuity to Abraham and his descendance (**Gen.22:15-18**). They have only retaken possession of it since 1948, having been expelled from their land in 73AD by the Roman legions. On and off, Israel has been at war with Islamic countries since its re-foundation.

Concerning Islam, since the death of their prophet Muhammad in 632 AD, its whole history has been an uninterrupted series of bloody conquests of Christian and other countries, in the Middle East, Europe and North Africa. Islam was also heavily engaged in the slave trade of Africans from the 17th to 19th centuries, selling millions of these unfortunates to European powers engaged in furnishing slaves to the USA and West Indies (See Chap.12 – The Reformation).

The Indian sub-continent was also defeated by Islam. While still under Muslim rule, it was appropriated by the East India Company of Britain in the 1700s, was taken over by the British Empire in 1858, and acquired independence from Britain only in 1947. Islamic Pakistan separated from Hindu India in 1948, and Bangladesh separated from the former in 1972.

Were God a Duality, there would also arise differences of opinion among his/their adepts, similar to political parties so prevalent in today's political systems. Even though Islam's Allah is One, yet the very serious differences between the two largest Islamic sects, the Sunnis and Shias, bolster the contention that in some way Allah is considered to be more like a cause of division than of unity, indeed a duality. A god of Duality, as being self-defeating from the outset, is therefore unacceptable.

To sum up, a Uni-Personal god who is Unity cannot be accepted, as its adepts could easily project their own wishes and interpret them to be those of their God and act accordingly, as in Judaism and Islam. Gods of Duality are also rejected, as shown above, considering the danger of competing opinions among adepts; and one of Multiplicity as well, as in Hinduism with its series of rebirths and unending reincarnations. In saying so, I respect those who hold to their beliefs in whichever god of their choice. *"In my Father's house, there are many rooms"*, said Our Lord (**Jn.14:2**), so there should be a place, one would hope, for all, even for those of vastly differing beliefs.

Having eliminated the possibilities of a God of Unity [as understood by Judaism and Islam], of Duality [though no group claims to hold this view], or Multiplicity [various Hindu sects hold to this, while explaining it as "avatars"], it remains to justify my faith in the Trinity, and here again the Illative Sense comes into play.

It is of course impossible to explain how One can be Three, and yet remain One, yet in the Catholic-Christian context it seems to hold together admirably, while admitting the impossibility of explaining this mystery. The Church teaches that the Three Persons are in fact a Unity, remaining One in **substance*, through their ***Hypostatic Union*.

The Church teaches that each Person has its specific function – the Father as Creator and Sustainer, the Son as Redeemer, the Spirit as Animator and Inspirer of the Church. The Holy Trinity should be seen as a God of circumincession, a term that expresses absolute divine intimacy and reciprocity among the Three Persons of the Godhead, which we can translate by the common words "Divine Love". With this there should be nothing more to object or reject. Yet it will always remain a mystery, *the* mystery, in fact.

Once a catechist in Africa wanted me to "explain" the Trinity to his group, so I tried to do it in this way. "A man wants to build a house, so he has the idea in his mind, how many rooms he has to plan for, the quantity of bricks, the season of rain and sun to plan for the time for building. So, he does everything according to plan. The ground is cleared, the bricks are made, the house is built, the rooms prepared, the roof is covered, all is in good shape.

"Now", I asked the group, "can we understand this man to be like the Father in the Trinity, the house that he has built to be the result of his plan?" "Sure", they said, "and the house is the Son, but what about the Spirit?" said a bright spark. "Well",

I said, "the planning, the effort, the change of plans, of finding more bricks, water etc, that was the work of the Spirit, wouldn't you agree? The man had to work out all these details in his mind, didn't he?"

"Well, yes", was the general opinion. "Because", said I, "the plan that the man had had in his head, his plan, his house, his effort, are these physical things so very different from what he had in his mind? They are physical, but have come from a mental and spiritual idea. They are really different, but are they in opposition? Don't they work as one? Aren't they united?"

"Yes, Father, they are united, even though they are very different!", they said, and they left, happy to have had the Trinity "explained", an example taken from their own human and daily existence. Wow!

I still wonder what St Augustine would have thought of that. Or did he possess the Illative Sense?

Well, *did he?*

-o-o-o-o-o-o-o-

***Substance** – *(Metaphysics)*. Nothing tangible or perceptible, but meaning the essential nature, the inner reality, of any physical entity. (See <u>Chap.8 – Transubstantiation</u>).

****Hypostatic Union** *of the Trinity* – This is the term used by the Church to identify the Persons in the Trinity. A personal, individual, complete **substance** exists entirely in itself in each Person, which **substance** is incommunicable to the other two Persons. The Catholic-Christian concept of the Trinity is often described as being One God existing in three distinct hypostases/ personae/persons, united by circumincession, Divine Love.

-o-o-o-o-o-o-o-

In you, O Lord, I take refuge.
Be a rock of refuge for me,
A mighty stronghold to save me,
For you are my rock, my stronghold;
For your name's sake, lead me and guide me.

(Ps.30(31), vs.1-2)

-o-o-o-o-o-o-o-

CHAPTER **12**

The Reformation

An Attempt to Understand

With the possible exception of the small but influential groups of atheists – found mostly in countries of traditional Christianity - most people in the world believe in some form of life after death. Buddhists and Confucianists of the East – China, Korea, Vietnam, Thailand etc - and those of the Shinto of Japan are the main ones, believing in a form of natural human happiness after death, provided on how one has lived one's life. This includes their belief in series of Reincarnations over and over again, until one should accede to this form of beatitude. However, the majority of people believe in a god or gods which gives sense to their lives.

Hinduism and its sects, Jainism, Sikhism, Swami-Narayan, etc. has a multiplicity of "gods", but defends this, saying that these millions are merely projections (avatars) of the divine characters of the one God, Brahman, whose character is fundamentally unknowable to humanity. Their holy books are the Bhagavad Gita, Kama-Sutra, Granth Sahib, etc.

Muslims believe in a Uni-personal God called Allah, an ancient Eastern moon-god promoted by their prophet Muhammad to be the only god from the group of 365 gods once worshipped in the Kaaba, the cubic building in Makkah, by the ancient Arabs. The holy book of Islam is the Qur'an, but Muslims depend on the Hadith, the Sunna and the Sira of Muhammad (his doings and sayings) to explain the Qur'an, and to direct and regulate their lives. Islam began in 632AD following the death of Muhammad in Medina. The Sunni is their largest (95%) sect, but there are others, the Shia, Wahhabis, Druze, Khadjirites, Brotherhood, Ismailis, Alawites, etc.

Judaism believes in the one God, Yahweh, now referred to as Ha-Shem (the Name). Having rejected Jesus as the Messiah, Judaism is now separated into several sects across the world. Its adepts still refer to the Tanakh (Old Testament) as the authentic Bible, and continue to obey the 613 Laws of Moses (the Torah) as their rule of life.

Christianity is the faith of the believers in a Tri-Personal Almighty God – comprising the Father, the Son, and Holy Spirit – fully revealed by Jesus the Christ, Second Person of the Blessed Trinity, the One who is the fulfilment of the ancient Jewish prophecies, the Messiah. It is a world-wide missionary religion, beginning after the Ascension of Jesus into heaven around 33AD. The Catholic Church is the largest of the Christian groups, which, due to historical misfortunes, are now separated into 47,000 non-Catholic denominations (according to the 2018 estimate of the Gordon-Cornwell Evangelical Seminary in the USA). Jesus' Vicar on earth is the Pope in Rome, its holy book (in fact a little library of 73 books, in the Catholic version) is the Bible, which itself was preceded by Tradition, before its texts were organised and compiled by authoritative Church Councils. The largest separations of the then Church occurred in 1054 – separation by the Eastern Church - and in the 16th century, when the Reformation occurred.

Try as we may, we cannot get rid of the evident truth that we are heirs of past history. Everything we do, say, or live, in some way reflects what has gone on before. The electric switch, the books we read in hard copy or computer-style, the clothes we wear, the cars we drive, the planes we travel in, everything in fact, all are based on inventions, ideas, innovations, from before our time, some from very forgotten periods. We are in fact beneficiaries of those who preceded us, and if history has anything to say about this, we too will be the forerunners of those who will follow us.

We of the 21st century so far seem to be tame imitators of years gone by. Without belabouring the fact too heavily by receding too far behind, we have been preceded by the 19th and 20th centuries, by tremendous political changes, by impressive movements of peoples, and above all by wars which have threatened the very existence of our world, not just the countries in which they had been waged. The 19th century saw the start of the British Empire, the Franco-Prussian War, followed by the Boer War. In the 20th century with its development of aircraft, its 52 wars, its World War 1 which was a warning, followed by the end of the Ottoman Empire, World War ll, the first Atomic Bombs, the Cold War, the Korean and Vietnamese Wars, the Moon Landings, the collapse of the Soviet Union and the fall of the Berlin Wall, the sexual revolution from 1965- 1977, the Second Vatican Council, and the resurgence of Islam.

Those two 19th and 20th centuries were preceded by others which have formed them, which in their turn were formed by others before, and so on and so on. In this present inquiry the 16th century attracts our attention, and we ask, what happened in the two preceding centuries, so that the Reformation of the 16th could take place? What for instance had happened in the 14th and 15th centuries, which led up to the tremendous changes of the 16th, both religiously and politically? Were these changes based on philosophies, religion, politics, or a combination or combinations of all three? This paper is an attempt to understand the Reformation, the main event of the 16th century, which influences to this day our own 21st century.

<u>The main events of the 14th century, from 1300 to 1399.</u> (Dates and details are from several sources)

1300 – There was as yet no Protestantism; the Catholic Church was foremost in the West, the Orthodox in the East.

1303 – Pope Boniface died after being abducted by Philip lV of France.

1307 – The Muslims drove the Crusaders from the Middle East.

1274-1329 – Robert the Bruce got independence for Scotland from England.

1304-1377 – The travels of Ibn Battuta of Morocco, who went three times farther than Marco Polo.

1309-1377 – The Avignon papacy; the Pope had left Rome for several reasons.
    - Notable writers were – Chaucer (1343-1404), and Dante (1265-1321).
    -The beginning of the Ottoman Empire – Osman l (1258-1326)

1337 – Start of the 100-year War, the beginning of the separate identities of England and France.

1347-1351 – The ***Black Death** (Bubonic Plague from the East) killed 25 million in Europe alone.

1378 – The unity of the Catholic Church was shattered – three popes at once – the Great Schism begins.

1381 – ***John Wycliffe** (+1384) was dismissed for criticizing the Church. His followers became the Lollards.
-The Renaissance began in Italy, changes of modes of thought; primitive capitalism began.
-The Great Famine in Europe killed millions; climate change was the main factor.
-Tamerlane (Muslim) founded the Timurid Empire, caused the deaths of about 17 million people.

1391 – Tamerlane briefly captured Moscow, then retreated to Samarkand.

1399 – Tally - about 45 million in all were killed in the 14th century.

***John Wycliffe** (1320-1384) was the forerunner, the very seed-bed of the future Reformation. He was a priest, a scholastic philosopher, theologian, professor in the University of Oxford. He was upset at the privileged status of the clergy, which had bolstered their powerful role in England, and also the luxury and pomp of local parishes and their ceremonies. He also advocated translation of the Bible from Latin into English, and in 1382 completed his own translation. His followers, known as Lollards, followed his lead in advocating predestination, iconoclasm, and caesaropapism, while attacking the veneration of saints, the Sacraments, Masses for the deceased, Transubstantiation, monasticism, and the very existence of the Papacy. His writings in Latin greatly influenced the philosophy and teaching of the Czech reformer Jan Hus (c. 1369–1415). He also attacked the temporal rule of the clergy, the collection of annates, indulgences, and simony. Wycliffe argued that the Church had fallen into sin and that it ought therefore to give up all its property and that the clergy should live in complete poverty.

The tendency of the high offices of state to be held by clerics was resented by many of the nobles. Wycliffe had come to regard the scriptures as the only reliable guide to the truth about God, and maintained that all Christians should rely on the Bible rather than on the teachings of popes and clerics. He said that there was no scriptural justification for the Papacy.

Theologically, his preaching expressed a strong belief in predestination that enabled him to declare an "invisible church of the elect", made up of those predestined to be saved, rather than in the visible Catholic Church. It was Wycliffe who recognised and formulated one of the two major formal principles of the Reformation – the unique authority of the Bible for the belief and life of the Christian. He also advocated the dissolution of the monasteries. Then the English hierarchy proceeded against him. As Chancellor of the University of Oxford, some of his declarations were pronounced heretical. Of the 24 propositions attributed to Wycliffe without mentioning his name, ten were declared heretical and fourteen erroneous. In the years before his death in 1384 he increasingly argued for Scriptures as the authoritative centre of Christianity, that the claims of the Papacy were unhistorical, that monasticism was irredeemably corrupt, and that the moral unworthiness of priests invalidated their office and the Sacraments. The Council of Constance (1415-1418) held in Germany, declared Wycliffe a heretic and banned his writings, effectively both excommunicating him retroactively and making him an early forerunner of Protestantism.

The Council decreed that Wycliffe's works should be burned and his bodily remains removed from consecrated ground. This order, confirmed by Pope Martin V, was carried out in 1428. Wycliffe's corpse was exhumed and burned and the ashes cast into the River Swift, which flows through Lutterworth, in Lancashire, England. Because of the Black Death, (seen by Wycliff as God's judgement), <u>the mortality rate among the clergy had been particularly high</u>, and those who replaced them were, in his opinion, uneducated or generally disreputable.

*The Black Death (peaked from 1347-1351 in Europe): Figures for the death toll vary widely by area and from source to source, and estimates are frequently revised as historical research brings new discoveries to light. Most scholars estimate that the Black Death killed between 75 and 200 million people in the 14th century, at a time when the entire world population was still less than 500 million. it took nearly 80 years for population sizes to recover, and in some areas more than 150 years. From the perspective of many of the survivors, the effect of the plague may have been ultimately favourable, as the massive reduction of the workforce meant their labour was suddenly in higher demand. For many Europeans, the 15th century was a golden age of prosperity and new opportunities. Land was plentiful, wages high, and serfdom had all but disappeared. Because of their hygienic practices, Jewish communities were generally spared, but this caused the extermination of many Jewish communities, under suspicion of witchcraft. <u>The Black Death hit the monasteries very hard</u> because of their proximity with the sick who sought refuge there. This left a <u>severe shortage of clergy</u> after the epidemic cycle. Monks, nuns and priests were especially hard-hit since they cared for victims of the Black Death. Eventually the <u>losses were replaced by hastily trained and inexperienced clergy</u>, many of whom knew little of the rigours of their predecessors. New colleges were opened at established universities, the training process speeded up. The shortage of priests opened new opportunities for laywomen to assume more extensive and more important service roles in the local parish.

(Thus, we see that in the 14th century, there had been a movement, led by **John Wycliffe**, against the Church in many of its manifestations – the clergy, its teachings, its importance in secular life, its wealth. This movement was not generally followed by the ordinary people, who remained content with the Church as they knew it. This was to change later on).

<u>The main events of the 15th century</u> – (1400 – 1499).
(Dates and details are from several sources)

1406 – Ptolemy's geography was introduced in Europe, the Earth considered to be the centre of the known universe.

1413 – Wycliffe's followers, the Lollards, were suppressed by Henry V.

1415 – ***Jan Hus**, Czech reformer (1369-1415) was declared a heretic and burned (1415).

1431 – Joan of Arc, heroine of the 100-years war, burnt at the stake for witchcraft. She was later exonerated.

1439 – Unsuccessful attempts to reconcile the Catholic Church with the Orthodox; the separation had occurred in 1054.

1453 – Islam captured Constantinople, using European artillery and experts.
 - 41 Jews were burnt at the stake in Poland.

1455 – Johann Gutenberg perfected his type-setting printing press.
 - The Vatican Library began.

1456 – The Ottomans overran Athens, remained for 400 years. The Parthenon was turned into a mosque.

1469 – Ferdinand of Aragon wed Isabella of Castile.

1480 – Leonardo da Vinci (28 years) invented the parachute.

1482 – The Portuguese installed trading posts along Africa's "Gold Coast".

1483 – Birth of *Martin Luther in Germany.

1485 – Henry Tudor won Battle of Bosworth in War of the Roses. Became Henry Vll, father of Henry Vlll.

1492 – Ferdinand and Isabella retook Granada from the Muslims.
 - Columbus went westward.

1494 – Columbus used tribesmen as slaves.

1497 – *Pope Alexander Vl excommunicated *Savonarola.

1498 – Savonarola was burnt at the stake.

*Jan Hus – (1372 – 1415), was a Czech theologian and philosopher who became a Church reformer and an inspirer of Hussitism, a key predecessor to Protestantism. After **John Wycliffe**, the theorist of ecclesiastical reform, Hus is considered to be the second Church reformer, as he lived before Luther, Calvin, and Zwingli. He opposed many aspects of the Catholic Church in Bohemia, such as their views on ecclesiology, simony, the Eucharist, and other theological topics. Pope Alexander V excommunicated Hus. When the Council of Constance (1415-1418) in Germany assembled, Hus was asked to be there and present his views on the dissension within the Church. When he arrived, he was immediately arrested and put in prison. He was eventually taken in front of the Council and asked to recant his views. When he refused, he was put back in prison. On July 6, 1415, he was burnt at the stake for heresy against the doctrines of the Catholic Church.

The writings of Jan Hus against the selling of indulgences influenced Martin Luther and other early Protestant Reformers. It is incorrect to refer to Jan Hus as a Protestant, however, as he held to many Catholic beliefs despite his strong opposition to papal authority and the selling of indulgences. Jan Hus set a tremendous example of refusing to submit to any authority that violates the teaching of Scripture. In that example, he is to be remembered and followed.

(**Jan Hus** inveighed against the sale of indulgences as a means of finding funds for political reasons, against simony, corruption in Church circles, Church authority, and the Papacy, advocating the inerrancy of Holy Scripture. In this he followed Wycliffe, and can thus be reasonably considered as a foremost forerunner of the Reformation of the 16th century).

*Girolamo Savonarola – (1452-1498). Born of a noble family in Florence, Italy, he entered the Dominican Order, becoming a friar and priest. He was known for his prophecies of civic glory, the destruction of secular art and culture, and his calls for Christian renewal. He denounced clerical corruption, despotic rule, the exploitation of the poor, and advocated reform in the cities and convents of north Italy. He prophesied the coming of a biblical flood and a new Cyrus from the north who would reform the Church. King Charles Vll of France then invaded Florence, expelled the ruling Medici family and, urged on by Savonarola, declared Florence a "popular republic". Florence and Savonarola refused to join Pope Alexander Vl's League against the French, and for having refused to go to Rome to defend this position, he was excommunicated in 1497. Popular opinion turned against him, and the Church and civic authorities condemned, hanged and burned him and two other friars in the main square of Florence in 1498. Savonarola's religious ideas found a reception elsewhere. In Germany and Switzerland the early Protestant reformers, most notably Martin Luther himself, read some of the friar's writings and praised him as a martyr and forerunner whose ideas on faith and grace anticipated Luther's own doctrine of justification by faith alone. The present-day Catholic Church has considered his beatification.

[The above details of the 14th and 15th centuries plainly show that there was widespread <u>confusion in the Catholic Church</u> as to what should be her role as the proclaimer to the world of salvation through Jesus the Christ. This confusion was increased not only through her wealth, but also through the unhealthy importance the Church enjoyed in civic affairs, the holding of offices in government by the clergy, which were no doubt bought, and of course her influence in directing governmental affairs. This situation was further exacerbated by the lingering effects of the **Black Death (1347-1351)**, which had taken a great toll of the parish clergy and the monks in the monasteries where the sick had fled for care. There were fewer Bishops to fill the Dioceses and Archdioceses, and thus more than one Diocese fell into the hands of one Bishop, leading to corruption and a certain nepotism. <u>Many ill-prepared people were ordained as priests</u> for parish work, and were generally ignorant of parish responsibilities. These problems helped to prepare the ground for the Reformation].

***Pope Alexander VI (1431-1503)**. Born of the Spanish Borja (Borgia) family, his character and reign as Pope are supremely controversial and scandalous. He was Pope from 1492-1503, and sought above all in his foreign policy the most advantageous terms for his family. He fathered several children, his son Cesare recovered for him the submission of the duchies of Florence, Milan and Venice, and he was also involved in nepotism, accumulating great wealth through corruption.

He ordered the death of Savonarola, but avoided conflict between Spain and Portugal in South America by delimiting areas of occupation on the continent.

The Sad Situation in Europe

Such an accumulation of religious confusion and political problems only served to further the need for change in Europe, particularly in the German States, where the need for social change was lurking on the horizon. There were hundreds of small independent sovereigns, leading to great rivalry between the princely families. Serfdom still was the backbone of the social structure and economy of the State, primitive capitalism and humanistic tendencies were tending to remove popular acceptance of the Church's control of the country, especially as Rome saw Germany as one of its main sources of income. This came to a head with the preaching of an Indulgence in 1517 in favour of the rebuilding of St Peter's Basilica in Rome.

To understand Indulgences: Sin is remitted by the Sacrament of Pardon of the Church, instituted by Jesus himself (**Jn. 20:21-23**), but includes a "penance" or action which a sinner remains obliged to perform even when God's mercy has forgiven the person, (**Jn.8:1-11** – *"Go, and sin no more"*), meaning that an effort of change, of repentance, must be made. The "penance" may be the performance of an act of charity or of piety, a pilgrimage, fasting, or prescribed prayers. But this Indulgence of 1517 was unfortunately too much associated with a monetary payment for the remission of the sins of those in Purgatory, promulgated by

Johann Tetzel, the monk charged to collect the funds. This false promotion of remission of sins became a source of scandal, one of the main causes of the Reformation.

After the Reformation started, the Council of Trent (1546-1563) reformed the indulgence system, clarifying its erroneous associations].

*Martin Luther (1483-1546) - (Excerpts from *"A History of The Church"* by Fr. Philip Hughes)

Martin Luther was a Law student, but in 1505 he abruptly changed course. He had been on horseback in a wood when a violent thunderstorm threw him to the ground, and in terror he cried that he would become a monk if he lived through it. Although his vow was most probably invalid, the same year, 1505, the Augustinian Order in Erfurt accepted him as Novice just 15 days afterwards.

[At that time, there were no seminaries like those of today. To become a priest, one had to enter a monastery or be a student with a resident parish-priest to learn one's philosophy, theology, pastoral duties, etc. Today, Luther would not be accepted in a seminary, due to his impure motivation of a vow made in fear. The Council of Trent instituted the seminary system].

In just two years, in 1507, he was ordained priest, and only then began his theology studies, which lasted no longer than 18 months. According to Hartmann Grisar, S.J. (1845-1932), his foremost biographer, *"Luther was of a permanently melancholic character, fear-ridden, guilt-haunted, a natural depressive; a moody, highly-strung novice, with violent alterations of hope and despair, of joy and depression. His personal anxieties were the main activity of his inner life".*

Luther received his Bachelor's Degree in Theology in 1509, and at 29 received his Doctor's Degree. But his interest was not so much in Theology. He was artistic, a poet, musician, a fascinating lecturer, a man of impulse and creative imagination, and turned to mystical use of Holy Scripture to find answers to his problems. In this, the Cross has no place, and <u>he fell into the spiritual fallacy called **presumption**, believing himself to be "saved"</u>. Notwithstanding his many responsibilities in the Augustinian Order, his intensely active imagination never ceased to haunt him that he was doomed to eternal punishment. Acceptance of Jesus as his Saviour, the Cross, the supernatural virtues and the efficaciousness of sanctifying grace, were not his principal preoccupations, but rather <u>his conviction that God was both omnipotent and arbitrary</u> [as does Islam also].

<u>Luther could not accept the sanctifying grace of God as the answer</u> to his spiritual problems, as God was essentially not its agent. He taught that man by original sin was forever corrupted in his very being, therefore good works as necessary for salvation were but a sham, a mere blasphemy. <u>He thus discarded the Sacraments, the priesthood, works of penance and petitionary prayer, even the Church. For him, **"Faith alone"** is the very touchstone of salvation</u>, it became his utter conviction. He thus presented to the Catholic world a new concept of Christianity, and gave the following as his active principles in his pamphlets: ***"Address to the nobility of the German nation"***, and ***"The Babylonian Captivity"***, in which:

1) He boldly attacked the hold of the Pope on Germany as a source of income. Annates (collections for Papal use) are to be abolished, and no more money must be sent out of Germany.

2) He satirised the Pope's claim to be the Holy Father of Christendom.

3) He offered to the ruling German classes a programme to make them supreme in German life, that it was Germany's destiny to rule mankind for mankind's greater good and happiness.

4) The Pope was denounced as the "real Turk", exploiting the simplicity of Germans.

5) The Church cannot need a visible Head, for it is itself an invisible thing.

6) The "power of the keys" is in reality the common possession of all the faithful.

7) No more foreigners must be appointed to German benefices.

8) All papal jurisdictions, spiritual or temporal, are to be abolished.

9) Pilgrimages to Rome must be abolished, along with religious guilds, indulgences, dispensations, holidays that are feast-days, and all Masses for the dead.

10) All believers are priests (Scripture says so), the clerical state and the hierarchy are mere human inventions, and have no place in the Church. Excommunication thus becomes a useless word.

11) It is the prince [the government] who must preside over the faithful, taking over Church property, even that of Rome.

12) The Emperor must be supreme; his imperial power is the heritage of the German race.

13) Priests and monks must free themselves from their vows and be allowed to marry.

14) The Papacy has been tyrannical over the Church of Christ; doctrine has been falsified.

15) The Sacraments are just three – Baptism, the Eucharist, and Penance.

16) The Eucharist is not a sacrifice; the Mass is simple devilish wickedness.

In his *"Liberty of a Christian man"* Luther presents his principal doctrine – that **Faith alone is needed for justification**, that without this faith nothing avails. There was no obligation on the justified believer to do good works. If he did any, that would be out of his own good will; not doing them would not entail any sin. Thus, according to Luther, even if *"we murder or fornicate thousands and thousands of times a day, faith in the glory of the Lamb that taketh away the sins of the world"*, saves the justified one. [The sin of Presumption seems never to have occurred to Luther, lacking the proper theology]

Such a principle shows a fundamental break between Faith and State Law. The State therefore becomes necessary as God's agent, for the work of ruling mankind and keeping it from growing morally worse. It is divinely authorised to punish man for his infractions of morality, decided and proclaimed by the State. The State therefore becomes Authority, and Authority is always right; the fact of punishment is proof of guilt. The State thus becomes a policeman, which is a theory that will dominate the political thought of all the Reformers. This continues to today; the Church being limited to the spiritual only.

This theory of Luther is akin to that of Machiavelli, but is more effective. For Luther, <u>man's</u> nature is totally corrupted by sin, his <u>will is not free</u>, and therefore the will of the prince [the government] is the will of the Almighty. Thus, <u>Luther denied the existence of natural law</u>, and man would have no right to choose, but must merely obey the will of the State, which becomes the substitute for God. The duty of the Christian is to submit to whatever is ordained for him. <u>The State is therefore freed from the control of Christian morality</u>, in the very name of Christian revelation! The State therefore has a moral and religious character, rendering the Church needless as a public thing. The Church thus becomes enemy of the State, which now becomes an agent for the reform of religion, making it a kind of church.

Before the start of the Reformation, although there had always been areas of disagreement and conflicts where the rights of the State and the Church tended to touch, no State had ever contested the principle that the Church, within its own sphere, was as truly sovereign as the State itself. It is this sovereign independence of religion as a visible public power, that Luther attacks and destroys, by denying the validity of the traditional distinction between the two authorities. His theory is that <u>the State is absolute by divine right</u>, but <u>the Church is invisible and purely spiritual</u>. It is therefore the business of the prince to care for morality and general good order, as the Church has no external authority, and cannot determine laws and enforce them. For in all such matters it is now the State which will now function.

<u>This eventually leads to the liberalisation and secularisation of society, the determination and control of man's morality by the State in matters of marriage, worship, and ritual. As temporal</u>

guardian of the divine law, the State is the only legitimate authority that the world should know. In other words, the former right of the Church to determine the right and wrong of moral choices no longer operates, the State is the divine arbiter of all. Man, not God, has become the centre of what religion should mean – man's need of God undetermined by purely human decisions. [Without the Sacraments of the Church, denied by Luther, man becomes forever locked within himself, as his life is no longer grafted onto the Divine life of God].

Luther's initial great victory began to be checked by the States in Europe which rejected his theories, and to this day has produced the effect that in Europe and throughout the world, Christianity has been divided into Protestant and Catholic factions, whose adherents no longer know, nor understand, nor are interested to examine, the causes for their divisions. Nor are they interested to examine the intention of Jesus on coming into this world, which had remained sacrosanct until the 16th century. Besides, the passage of time, political decisions, family cohesion and interests, and national histories, have all combined to cause a terrible break in man's ability to think and choose objectively. The huge and seemingly insoluble problems endemic at the present moment in the countries of traditional Christian civilisation are clearly due to a basic denial of their Catholic-Christian past. It is to be hoped that Luther's personal demons, which served only to divide and destroy Western civilisation, will be put to rest by clear and objective thinkers of the future, that the experience of the Reformation will serve to remind man of the need of meaning to life. As Jesus said *"I am the Way, the Truth, and the Life"* (**Jn. 14:6**). Other ways have been tried, but have been found wanting, all having denied the God-given authority of the Catholic Church.

Opening the windows of the debate

Martin Luther was indeed the spark which started the conflagration, and was followed by Melanchthon, Calvin, Zwingli, Bucer, Knox, and Henry Vlll. Apart from these seven, there were 279 others, all leaders in the parishes and dioceses, who joined ranks with them, publicly announcing their adhesion to the movement, no doubt because the suspicions of Church corruption were so widespread. Even though careful enquiries were possibly not made, the opportuneness of linking themselves to a popular movement, with the possibility of eventual gain, most probably stimulated their enthusiasm. As St. Paul said it so rightly *"People will be avid for the latest novelty"…..they will turn to myths"* (**2 Tim.4:3-4**).

Luther's Teaching

The uniquely characteristic element of Luther's teaching is the doctrine of **justification by faith alone**. Put more simply, this means that the superabundant merits of Our Lord Jesus Christ, alone and by themselves, without our cooperation, assure the eternal salvation of man, so that one may lead a life of sin in this world with neither remorse of conscience nor fear of God's justice. For Luther, the voice of conscience was not that of grace, but rather that of the Devil! For this reason, he wrote to a friend that a man vexed by the Devil should occasionally *"drink more abundantly, gamble, entertain himself, and even commit some sin out of hatred and spite for the Devil, so that we may not give him an opportunity to disturb our consciences with trifles. The whole Decalogue should be erased from our eyes and our souls".*

The incitement to sin given in a letter to Melanchthon on August 1, 1521, is perhaps even more categorical: ***"Be a sinner, and sin strongly (esto peccator et pecca fortiter), but believe and rejoice even more firmly in Christ, the conqueror of sin, of death, and of the world. During this life, we have to sin. It is sufficient that, by the mercy of God, we know the Lamb who takes away the sins of the world. Sin will not separate us from Him, even though we were to commit a thousand murders and a thousand adulteries per day".*** <u>This doctrine is so bizarre that even Luther himself could scarcely manage to believe in it:</u> ***<u>"There is no religion in the whole world that teaches this doctrine of justification; I myself, even though I teach it publicly, have a great difficulty in believing it privately."</u>***

Luther was excommunicated by Pope Leo X in January 1521, and three months later, at the Diet of Worms he was declared a heretic and outlaw by the Holy Roman Emperor, Charles V. He was then abducted by the troops of the Elector of Saxony, Frederick lll, and kept in his castle of Wartburg for almost a year. He used this time to translate the New Testament and write his tracts. In 1525 he married Katharina von Bora, a former nun, and had 6 children.

In 1534 his complete translation of the Bible appeared, making it more accessible to the laity, an event that had a tremendous impact on both the Church and German culture. It fostered the development of a standard version of the German language, adding several principles to the art of translation. In two of his later works, Luther expressed antagonistic, violent views towards Jews, and called for the burnings of their synagogues and their deaths. His rhetoric was not directed at Jews alone, but also towards Catholics, Anabaptists, and non-trinitarian Christians.

Finally, Luther published many tracts and pamphlets during his life, which allowed the rapid spread of the Protestant faiths, but it was the invention of the printing-press in 1455 by Gutenberg which facilitated the dissemination of his works throughout Europe and the northern countries of Sweden, Denmark and Norway, all of which took to Lutheranism.

Martin Luther, schismatic and heresiarch, died in 1546 with Pope Leo X's excommunication still effective.

Results of the Reformation

1) Europe, arena of the upheaval of the Reformation, is now in 2020 considered to be post-Christian. The churches are emptying, attendance is derisory, secularism and atheism are rampant. Although the Catholic Church had kept intact the message of Jesus up to the 16th century, the past 500 years have proven that without her authority under the protection of the Spirit promised by Our Lord (**Jn.16:4-15**), evil may have the chance to prevail. In 2018, an estimated 47,000 non-Catholic Christian sects [cf. estimate of the Gordon-Conwell Evangelical Seminary in the USA] use the Bible alone as their sole source of Authority, divorced from the Traditions of the Catholic Church. These Traditions had preceded the compilation of the Bible itself, which was completed finally by the Church Councils of **Hippo** (393 AD), and those of **Carthage** (397 and 419 AD), all of which took place in North Africa. These Councils had affirmed the 46-books Canon of the Old Testament, but it took Luther in the 16th century to leave out 7 of them, following the Rabbis of Jamnia.

2) Free and individual interpretation of the Bible is practised, and the principal tenet of Lutheran teaching – one is presumed to be

saved, justified, by Faith *alone* – (known as *fideism*), is accepted by all these 47,000 groups (as above). [This the Church considers to be the sin of Presumption - One considers oneself to be saved, one does not even need the Pardon of the Church, as instituted by Jesus himself (**Jn. 20:21-23**)]. (Ref. **Ps.19(18), v.13**)

3) The Church is considered to be the Whore of Babylon by many of the Separated Brethren, the priesthood of an ordained individual to be a sham; instead the priesthood belongs to all believers. There is no cult of Mary nor of the Saints, Jesus alone is the object of Protestant devotion. This "belief" of the Separated Brethren seems to be mainly sentimental. They practise the faith occasionally, but do not take the words of Jesus seriously, preferring to see many merely as symbolic suggestions – the One Church, the Priesthood, the Pardon of sins, the Eucharist.

4) The Seven Sacraments are considered spurious, but Baptism, Penance, and the "Lord's Supper" are practised by many, each being interpreted differently. The Eucharist is merely a symbol for most, the Catholic Mass is blasphemy, and the institution of the Papacy on Simon, renamed "Peter" by Jesus, (**Mt.16:18-20, and Jn.21:15-17**)) is non-historical.

(See, Chap. 16 – The Rock).

5) The Church is no longer the visible, One and true Church founded by Christ (**Mt.16:13-20**). Rather, it has become an "invisible church of all believers". Such teaching originated in the "Branch Theory", in which there are three authentic churches – the Catholic, Orthodox, and Anglican, but some also include the Oriental churches. This theory was started by William Palmer of Oxford (1803-1885).

6) Although the practice of Usury – basically, Interest on loans, including Compound Interest – had been prohibited by the

Church, a form of primitive capitalism had been practised by the monasteries. Once the Reformation had occurred, these prohibitions no longer prevailed, and the break-up of Europe into political factions resulted in uncontrolled capitalism, which in turn resulted in the formation of the great banking Houses, rivalry between richer and poorer countries, armed conflicts, and hardening of relations between former Catholic countries into blocs of power and influence.

7) Although slavery had been practised from immemorial times in many countries, yet <u>the rejection of Church authority and control</u>, the discovery of new lands in the West by Columbus and the need for many hands to cultivate there, <u>gave rise to the Atlantic Slave Trade</u>, practised by the so-called Christian, formerly Catholic countries - France, Spain, Germany, Denmark – through which captive Africans were bought from African chiefs and from Muslims in slave-markets around the continent. <u>Even the condemnation of this trade by the Popes went unheeded</u>, until certain groups of the Separated Brethren, the Quakers, and by Wilberforce, etc – forced their Governments to end this terrible trade, in the 1830s, for Britain and most of their colonies, and in 1865, for the United States. It still continues here and there under different forms.

8) Although the African slave trade had ended, yet a simmering covetousness remained, because Africa was still relatively untouched. Colonisation of the weak by the powerful had always existed, but it was Bismarck, the [Protestant] Prussian Iron Chancellor of Germany, who did something about Africa. At his Berlin Conference (1885) the African continent was divided-up for **colonisation** between Britain, France, Germany, Portugal, Italy, and Belgium, the powerful countries at that time, which also retained their hold on former colonies in the West. <u>The Church's authority, low since the 16th century, was ignored</u>.

Abuses occurred (the Congo Free State under Belgium, Namibia, under Germany, Mozambique, under Portugal, Ethiopia-Somalia, under Italy, boundary divisions of African tribes under Britain and France); but there were **improvements** also (slavery was abolished, infrastructures developed [governments, democracy], education and health, were prioritised). Colonisation receded as independence was gained from 1947 (India), and other countries in the 1960's, though many inter-statal improvements are still needed.

9) As said above, due to the rise of usury and certain banking practices formerly prohibited by the Catholic Church, the Reformation gave impetus, with the introduction of new inventions, to the rise of the Industrial Revolution. This brought about uncontrolled capitalism, which in turn brought about the terrible reaction of Communism and the upholding of workers' rights. This fostered the belligerence of the Protestant states of Germany, the Prussian dominance there, and eventually WW1 (1914-1918), followed by an uninterrupted series of 52 wars in the 20th century, many being of Communist origin. The Spanish Civil War (1937-1939) followed, then WW2 (1939-1945). This was seen by Germans as payback for the victimisation they considered they had suffered under the Treaty of Versailles in 1919, the loss of their territories, and, according to Hitler, Jewish betrayal. World-wide tensions and wars between States professing ideological differences followed – the Cold War, the Vietnamese and Korean wars, the latter being still unresolved in 2020.

10) Being involved in world affairs as always, the Catholic Church has also been severely influenced by the changes occurring worldwide. About 72% of the Catholic youth in the USA now believe that the Eucharist is only symbolic, that there are no obligations to be observed, e.g. that of Sunday Mass, Confession at least once yearly at Easter-time, support of the Church, etc. The

Sexual Revolution of 1965 -1977 has also had a baleful influence on Catholic youth, many of whom have become agnostic or atheist, the moral/sexual life of many becoming merely recreational or pure pastime. Marriages in Church have diminished, babies remain unbaptised, divorces have sky-rocketed, and more than one generation of young people will be considered anti- or non-Catholic for the coming years - if present trends continue.

(See <u>Chap. 20 – The Catholic Family</u>)

[From "A History of the Church" by Fr. Philip Hughes (Sheed & Ward, 1947, and other sources].

-o-o-o-o-o-o-o-

Final Assessment of the post-Reformation situation.

1) Many mistakes have been made by each side through the centuries, concerning the debates about the historicity of the Papacy, the priesthood of individuals or that of all believers, the Sacraments, the cults of the Saints, of the Virgin Mary, the roles of Faith and Works, etc.

2) Several factors have entered into the reasons causing the continuation of the break-up of the Church founded by Jesus – politics, family adhesions, financial considerations, historical hurts – each of which should be understood and remedied.

3) Has the world become better off since the mid-16th century? Is it a happier place, and are people happier in general? Is it a world of security, where the family can prosper, taking into account the needs of others who may differ? Opinions….

4) Taking the world as a planet confided to our care, have we respected this injunction from the Creator? Opinions…..

5) Former Catholic countries, now largely Protestant, are now abandoning their ties to the teachings of the Reformers and to the sect of their choice. They are now becoming paganised, and the sects have grown exponentially. What is more, there are serious risings of Satanism and anti-Catholicism in various parts of the world, even in Protestant countries, exactly as Jesus had predicted (**Jn.15:18-27**; **16:1-4**). The Protestant movement is barely holding on, the churches are emptying, and in general it is clear that the past 500 years have not faced up to the expectations of the Reformers. The young of the Separated Brethren couldn't care less for the Bible and being saved, they save themselves by their own means, be it by drugs, concubinage, delinquency, and associated anti-social activities.

6) The Catholic Church has also suffered terribly from the Reformation, showing the influence of Protestantism. Except in the countries of Mission, Church marriages and their hopeful results have declined, divorce, concubinage, and attendant social aberrations have sky-rocketed. Catholic youth has also been affected, to their parents' dismay.

(See Chap.20 – The Catholic Family)

7) Where is the present inter-religious effort to discover just how re-unification can proceed, so that there may be *"one flock, one Shepherd"* as desired and foretold by Our Saviour? (**Jn.10:16**)? Success or not of Ecumenism…..

Addendum: There are those who may accuse the Church of having added to the "deposit of faith" certain teachings foreign to her origins. It is certain that the Apostles, sent to the nations (**Mt.28:19**), carried the very simple message of Jesus, his death, Resurrection, and his promise to return, along with his extraordinary teachings of a loving God-the-Father; but they did not know certain dogmas of the Church, decided by Councils through the centuries. These were in fact guaranteed by the Spirit to be sent (**Jn.16:12-13**), and realised at Pentecost (**Acts 2:1-12**).

Jesus had also said that new teachings would arrive in the Church's development (**Mt.13:52** – "***Every scribe*** [Church theologian] ***who has been trained for the kingdom of heaven*** [Serious instruction is necessary] ***is like a householder*** [the hierarchy] ***who brings out of his treasure*** [the Old and New Testaments, Church history, theological investigations] ***what is new and what is old***" [old = Deeper understanding of the Old Testament, etc].

Such "new" teachings would be the dogmas decided by Church Councils and Popes, depending on theological and historical authenticity – the Divinity of Jesus (**1ˢᵗ Nicaea, 325**); God as a Trinity of Persons (**1ˢᵗ Nicaea, 325**); the Virgin Birth (**1ˢᵗ Nicaea 325**); Mary's Perpetual Virginity (**Constantinople 533**); Mary the Mother of God (**Ephesus 431**); Papal Infallibility (**Vatican I, 1868**); Immaculate Conception of Mary (**Pius IX, 1854**); Assumption of Mary (**Pius XII, 1950**).

> For the Lord will not forsake his people,
> He will not abandon his heritage;
> For justice will return to the righteous,
> And the upright of heart will follow it.
>
> (Ps.94(93), vs. 14-15)

–o-o-o-o-o-o-o–

CHAPTER **13**
The Bible Alone

Sola Scriptura

<u>*Sola Scriptura*</u>: To be saved, one should depend on, and by guided only, by the writ of Holy Scripture, the Bible [Luther].

<u>**Question**</u>: Seeing that this was the fundamental teaching by Martin Luther from 1520 onwards, aided by the use of Gutenberg, whose press had printed in 1455 the first book in the West, the Bible, one may ask, - if Salvation came only through Luther's use of the Bible he had translated from the Vulgate into the German language, and considering all the millions of people who presumably had not used the Bible from the Ascension of Christ, around 33 AD, until Luther's discovery of *Sola Scriptura*, would all these folk have been condemned to eternal punishment through ignorance of *Sola Scriptura*, and how would *Sola Scriptura* then explain the kindness of God, who is Love itself? (**1Jn.4:8,16**). In fact, did Luther ever even consider how the antecedent histories of countless millions could have been affected by his "discovery?" They had no idea of *sola scriptura*, being accustomed to a *teaching* Church, with *authority* to do so (**Mt.16:13-20**; **28:20**)

To answer the problem of *sola scriptura*, one should be aware of how and where the Bible originated. The following is based on the book *"Where we got the Bible"*, by Rt. Rev. Henry G. Graham (1911, followed by 17 re-printings).

1) Before Johann Gutenberg of Germany printed the first book in history (1455) to be used for reading by the general public, which was the Latin Vulgate Bible of St Jerome (4th c.AD), which Christian sacred books were there in existence? <u>The first was the Jewish Septuagint</u> (70 rabbis in Alexandria had translated the Jewish Old Testament from Hebrew to Greek because of Hebrew disappearing. Greek had become the *lingua franca* of the Mediterranean world). <u>The second was the Latin Vulgate of Jerome</u>. Ordinary folk had no Bibles (no printed books as yet were in existence), each was copied by hand in the monasteries. Vulgate Bibles were much too expensive, and were chained for reading in churches, so as to avoid theft. The Church taught by word of mouth (**Mt.28:18-20**), which was <u>a command to go and teach</u>, not go and read. <u>The Church existed before the written word became common</u>. There was no popular reading of the Bible as is possible today, and as no microphones existed, in the churches podiums were placed high in the centre, to ensure hearing by the faithful.

2) The Gospels and Epistles were written to specific groups of people to address questions of morality, faith etc, not to give a complete exposition of the Faith, i.e. the Church herself had existed before these were written. Jesus had guaranteed that by the Spirit she would not fall into error, that she would be led to all truth, and that it would be gradual, as the Apostles were still too "young" to understand (**Jn.14:16-17, 26; 15:26; 16:12-14**).

3) For many years the various books were not in one volume, as we know it today, but copies of the Gospels and Epistles were circulating all around the known world, each hand-copied. The

Council of Carthage (397 AD) decided on the names of the books to form the Bible, and this decision was sent to Rome for confirmation. For its part, Rome was able to reject the spurious and uncanonical ones (e.g. the gnostic writings), and many people were martyred, unwilling to give up the canonical ones due to the Roman persecutions. The Council's decision was confirmed also by the **Councils of Florence (1442) and Trent (1546-1563)**. These decisions were attacked by the Protestant Reformers in the 16th century.

4) The Catholic Church claims the authority to have decided on the composition of the biblical books (**Mt.16:13-20**), and alone to have the authority to give its true meaning. Claims of the present-day "reformers" are groundless as to the authenticity of the Bible, as their founders seem to have followed the Rabbis in *Jamnia in not accepting those of the Septuagint. Thus, several of the books – Tobias, Baruch, Judith, Wisdom, Ecclesiasticus, Maccabees 1 & 2, 7 chapters of Esther, 66 verses of the 3rd chapter of Daniel, were left out by Luther. Those of Hebrews, Jude, James and Revelation were spared. (Today, all of the original Aramaic documents have been found, either in Masada or in the Dead Sea Scrolls, and are included in the NRSV (Catholic Editions) of the Bible). But they had always been included in the Septuagint.

5) All of the original documents – and perhaps some others by the Apostles and Paul – were destroyed in the Roman persecutions (except for rare pieces e.g.* Ryland's of St John, below). All were copied on perishable papyrus, and once copied, it was not thought necessary or possible to keep the originals. The Church was there to keep teaching and explaining, as the copies were considered good enough.

6) The Catholic Church is oblivious to charges that the originals have disappeared, as the Church itself was always there to teach.

She <u>did not depend on the Bible alone</u>. The earliest manuscripts of the New Testament are from around 300 AD, while copies of the scrolls of ancient authors, (e.g. Herodotus, Thucydides, who lived 400 BC) are only from around the 11th century AD. It is absurd to accept the latter while rejecting the former.

7) The ages of the copies are often interpreted by dating in the margins or by changes in handwriting fashion. Divisions of the Bible into chapters and verses were probably done by Stephen Langton, Archbishop of Canterbury (1150-1258), or by Denys the Short, a monk. The illustrations in mediaeval times attest to the love and respect for the texts. Many faults came thru age, bad eyesight, forgetfulness, inattention, bad hearing, or "glosses" e.g. the prayer from the **_Didache_** – a first-century prayer added to the Lord's Prayer by the Reformers. Even though there may have been errors by copyists, it is the Church which guaranteed the truth from the start.

8) The so-called "Dark Ages" were "light" compared to what has been happening to Western Civilisation in the 20th and beginning of the 21st Centuries. In mediaeval times Universities and the great Cathedrals were built, there was Scholasticism, the great theologians, the defence of Christianity against. Islam. The 20th century has given us innumerable wars (over 52, in fact), the Holocaust, the Bomb, Islamic terrorism, unregulated capitalism, etc. Mediaeval Monks and Nuns in the monasteries and convents dedicated their lives to copying the sacred texts, expertly copied and illustrated, e.g. Book of Kells and devotional books, among others. Each monastery had its own Bible for public use. Perishable papyrus had given way to vellum (calves' skins) for copying, and double-copying gave rise to "palimpsests" – erasure and re-writing on vellum. Inks were invented, pens were of many sorts. Ignorance or prejudice among present-day "reformers" downplay

the importance of the mediaeval age in keeping the Bible alive from earliest times.

9) The Constitutions and Rules of monasteries made obligatory the knowledge and meaning of the Scriptures by the monks. Even ordinary folk used scriptural phrases in ordinary life, as shown by the many Wills, bills of sale, contracts, legal letters, sacred plays, stained-glass windows, from that time. There is today a danger of literary idolatry – worshipping the letter while neglecting the spirit. The Catholic Church has never been guilty of despising Holy Scripture.

10) Spoken Latin was commonly understood in the Middle Ages, most people spoke it. English also was spoken, but was not printed until after 1455. Latin was a living language. Many mediaeval Bibles were destroyed by wars and invasions – Danes, Normans, Muslims etc, or by theft, climate, negligence, destruction of libraries and books for the inlays of gold and precious stones, e.g. Henry VIII's suppression of the monasteries during the Reformation, destruction of the library of Alexandria by Muslims, (who also destroyed the Indian University of Nalanda in the early 12th century).

11) In the Middle Ages many countries had translations of the Bible in their national languages. This was so in Whitby in England in the 7th century. St Bede commented on this, and several other translations existed from 1066, 1150, 1250, 1349, 1611, and, (according to Protestant testimony), the Bible was translated into Saxon. <u>Wycliffe was NOT the first to translate the Bible into English</u>. Luther's Bible in German came out in 1520, but before 1520 there were 104 editions of the Bible in Latin, 9 in German before Luther's birth, and 27 before Luther's Bible appeared. In Italy there were 40 editions of the Bible in Italian

before the first Protestant version appeared, etc, as was the case in France, Hungary, Bohemia.

12) The Catholic Church has the duty and right to protect the Scriptures e.g. Wycliffe's version (1382) was incorrect and false, not because it was a Bible, as "reformers" maintain. His followers the Lollards continued to despise the Mass, celibacy, prayers for the dead, veneration of images, the Sacraments etc. He was condemned as being heretical and blasphemous, as was Nicholas of Hereford. Wycliffe died of a stroke after Mass (1384). In France (12th and 13th centuries) the Waldenses and Cathars (Albigenses) were also condemned for false teaching on marriage, Baptism, Resurrection etc. In England Tyndale (b.1484) published his Bible in 1525, in Worms (Germany) during the Lutheran upheaval. It was full of Lutheran heresies, influence and errors. The Tyndale Bible was burnt and denounced by Henry VIII himself (1543).

13) <u>Many Bibles came out in the reign of Henry VIII</u> – Coverdale's, Taverner's (1539), Cranmer's and Cromwell's, the Geneva [Breeches] Bible, from Calvin. In England there were the Bishop's Bible, Unrighteous Bible, Bug Bible, Treacle Bible, Pearl Bible, Polyglot Bible (17th century).

14) The Catholic Church published its own authorised version in English from Douai in France (1582), translated from the Vulgate of St Jerome, with several translators. Then came the English Haydock Bible (1811), the Jerusalem Bible in English from 1966, and several onwards.

From all the above considerations, it is quite impossible and absurd to maintain that Luther's *Sola Scriptura* should be the sole judge of man's hope to arrive at heavenly bliss. It is clear that the Bible was honoured and kept alive through the centuries of Christendom by the Catholic Church, notwithstanding the persecutions, invasions, manifold destructions, and malice of the so-called "Reformers". Rather, these latter should be re-termed "Deformers" by impartial observers. What is more, Luther's attempt to break with the Catholic Church has succeeded, even beyond his wildest expectations. What began as his personal obsession has now blossomed into over 47,000 non-Catholic Christian sects *(estimation of the Gordon-Conwell Protestant Evangelical Seminary in the U.S., 2018),* each believing in its own understanding of *Sola Scriptura*. This in itself has led to the dire condition of western civilisation from the 1500s onwards. Notwithstanding its great scientific advances, the terrible loss of common humanity and unity should be put squarely at the feet of Martin Luther, the original dissident, heresiarch and schismatic, uncritically followed by millions in the world today.

-o-o-o-o-o-o-

***Jamnia** – or Yahnev near Jaffa on the western coast of modern Israel, is supposed to have been the place where the leading Rabbis of Jerusalem had gathered after the destruction of the Temple in 70 AD. They had taken with them the majority of the books which they had collected in their flight from the Holy City, and as usual were involved in discussing which were the books considered as worthy to be included in their Canon of Scripture. At that moment there was as yet no fixed Jewish Canon of the Old Testament (the Tanakh), which consisted of three groups, the Law of Moses, the Prophets, and the Writings (Psalms and others, including Ecclesiastes, Song of Songs, etc).

Heinrich Gretz (Jewish scholar in Germany in the 1800s) proposed that it was in Jamnia around 90 AD that a "Council" took place to decide on the authenticity of these books. Before that proposition there had not been any mention of Jamnia, and neither in the Mishnah, a collection of oral traditions debated by the Rabbis, nor in the Talmud, was there any mention nor clear evidence of a "Council" of Jamnia.

This proposal of Gretz was adopted by a Protestant scholar named Ryle in 1892, but another named Lewis in 1930 showed that there was no reason to adopt Jamnia, as there had not been any mention of this place in the Jewish discussions on the Apocrypha. It should therefore to be considered as a myth.

But the Catholic Church had no problem concerning its acceptance of the 46 Jewish books in the Old Testament, the Jewish Tanakh. All these books had been translated into Greek around 250 BC by the Rabbis in Alexandria, believed to have been about 70 in all. It had been necessary to translate into Greek, as Hebrew as a *lingua franca* was disappearing at that time. Greek had become the language of the people, all due to the conquests of Alexander the Great.

Jesus and the writers in the early Church were very aware of the Septuagint, as it was called, and used it frequently.

Nevertheless, the Jewish books in discussion in ancient times - Tobias, Baruch, Judith, Wisdom, Ecclesiasticus, Maccabees 1 & 2, 7 chapters of Esther, 66 verses of the 3rd chapter of Daniel – have not been included in the Jewish Canon to this day, and this has been followed by not being included either in the King James and other Protestant editions.

*Papyrus 52: A Fragment of John's Gospel

This small fragment of St. John's Gospel, less than nine centimetres high and containing on the one side part of verses 31-33, on the other of verses 37-38 of chapter xviii is one of the collections of Greek papyri in the John Rylands Library, Manchester. It was originally discovered in Egypt, and may come from the famous site of Oxyrhynchus (Behnesa), the ruined city in Upper Egypt where <u>Grenfell and Hunt</u> carried out some of the most startling and successful excavations in the history of archaeology; it may be remembered that among their finds of new fragments of Classical and Christian literature were the now familiar "Sayings of Jesus". The importance of this fragment is quite out of proportion to its size, since it may with some confidence be dated in the first half of the second century A.D., and thus ranks as the earliest known fragment of the New Testament in any language. It provides us with invaluable evidence of the spread of Christianity in areas distant from the land of its origin; it is particularly interesting to know that among the books read by the early Christians in Upper Egypt was St. John's Gospel, commonly regarded as one of the last of the books of the New Testament. Like other early Christian works which have been found in Egypt, this Gospel was written in the form of a codex, i.e. book, not of a roll, the common vehicle for pagan literature of that time.

-o-o-o-o-o-o-o-

O, sing to the Lord a new song
For he has done marvellous things;
His right hand and his holy arm
Have gotten him victory.
The Lord has made known his victory,
He has revealed his vindication
In the sight of the nations;
He has remembered his steadfast love and faithfulness
To the house of Israel
All the ends of the earth have seen
The victory of our God.

(Ps.98, vs 1-3-

-o-o-o-o-o-o-o-o-

CHAPTER 14
Faith Alone

<u>Sola Fide</u> or <u>*Fideism</u>

Fideism – This means "Trust based on faith rather than on Reason" (Collins English Dictionary)

<u>Sola Fide</u>: This is the second tenet in the teaching of Martin Luther, heresiarch and destroyer of the religious and political unity of Europe, originator of the 16th century Reformation, at a time of sorely-needed reforms of the Catholic Church. Basically, it means that Faith alone is necessary for Salvation i.e. to be saved, one needs faith alone; thus, without it one cannot be saved, allowed entry into God's Kingdom. Such a person is condemned by his own lack of faith in God, and depends more on his own personal efforts and particular judgment to have faith, rather than faith as a free gift from God.

For <u>Luther</u>, a ***"fear-ridden, guilt-haunted, natural depressive"*** person (See <u>Chap.12 – The Reformation</u>), Faith was so important that he <u>added the word "**alone**"</u> [*allein*] after the last word in **Romans 1:17** in his translation into German from the Latin Vulgate, making it "<u>Man is justified by faith ***alone***</u>", which is non-biblical and also a serious theological aberration. <u>This was</u>

later removed from Lutheran Bibles, but the word has stuck in the collective memory of the "reformers" to this day.

The Catholic Church can agree with Luther to a point. Faith is necessary for salvation, but it is also a free gift from God, and can be asked for in fervent prayer. However, there is a difference of opinions between and Lutheranism and the Church concerning others of non-Christian faith. Here the Council Vatican ll has given clear rulings in the Declaration *"Nostra Aetate"* (1965), proclaiming that faith in the saving power of Christ as the only one in which the ultimate hope of humanity can possibly rest, His Cross being sign of the universal love of God and source of all grace. She also proclaims that universal fraternity excludes every form of discrimination, coming from whatever source:

1) Non-Christians means Hindus, Buddhists, Shintoists, Confucianists, Animists – others, including atheists etc. The Church emphasises the common humanity of all peoples, respects the efforts of each group to find meaning in its beliefs (or lack of belief), as each group contains in itself a ray of truth which can help to enlighten humanity. Others are:

2) Islam. The Church esteems the Muslims, who 'claim descent from Abraham', belief in one God, and seek him by diverse means. They are encouraged to forget the sad history they share with the Church, to work with her to promote social justice, peace and liberty. *[Ancient Arabia knew nothing of Abraham, nor of Ishmael his illegitimate son by Hagar, Nestorian Christians had taught this to Muhammad)*

3) The Jews – the Church freely acknowledges the debt she owes to the Chosen People, from whom have come the Patriarchs and the Prophets, and from whom she has sprung. Although they have not, as a people, accepted Jesus as Messiah, yet the Church awaits the

day when all will invoke and serve the same God (**Zeph.3:9-20; Rom.11:31-32**). In the meantime, the Church deplores all forms of anti-Semitism, and encourages both to continue biblical and theological studies, as well as fraternal dialogue.

[[Luther wrote disparagingly of the Jews in ***"On the Jews and their lies",*** in a text used by <u>Adolf Hitler</u> to justify the Holocaust. <u>Concerning the Muslims</u>, Luther declared:

Anyone can easily observe that Mohammed is a destroyer of our Lord Christ and His kingdom, and if anyone denies concerning Christ, that He is God's Son and has died for us, and still lives and reigns at the right hand of God, what has he left of Christ? Father, Son, Holy Ghost, Baptism, the Sacrament, Gospel, Faith and all Christian doctrine and life are gone, and there is left, instead of Christ, nothing more than <u>Mohammed with his doctrine of works and especially of the sword. That is the chief doctrine of the Turkish faith</u> in which all abominations, all errors, all devils are piled up in one heap. Thus, the Turk is, in truth, nothing but a murderer or highwayman, as his deeds show before men's eyes. Now we have heard above what kind of man the Turk is, viz., a destroyer, enemy, and blasphemer of our Lord Jesus Christ, who, instead of the Gospel and faith, sets up his shameful Mohammed and all kinds of lies, ruins all temporal government and home-life, or marriage, and, since his warfare is nothing but murder and bloodshed, is a tool of the devil himself.]]

There are thus wide divergences between the views of the Church and those of Luther concerning both the Jews and the Muslims, as shown above.

The real problem between the Church and Luther concerns that of **Faith** and **Works**. Both would agree that **Work**s by itself is not a guarantee of salvation, although for the Church pure humanism and philanthropy would certainly count to the credit of the person in question, <u>acting in conscience</u> for humanity's benefit.

It seems to be unclear just what the position of present-day "reformers" would be, seeing that **Faith** would probably be absent, where **Works** may abound in the many philanthropic activities undertaken by the N.G.Os. and secular society.

<u>The Church's view</u> concerning **Faith** and **Works** can be seen in several Gospel texts- <u>"Law" meaning that of Moses.</u>

Mt.3:9-11 – the Faith of the Jews in Abraham was faulty in not producing <u>good fruit</u>, i.e. works.

Mt.5:16 – Let your light shine before others, that they may see your <u>good works</u>, and give glory to the Father.

Mt.7:12 – Following the "Law" [by Faith] is not enough. There must also be <u>good treatment</u> of others, i.e. works.

Mt.7:21-27- Faith in the Lord is not enough, <u>one must act</u> on it, i.e. works.

Mt.12:1-8 – Following the "Law" [by Faith] is not enough. <u>There must be mercy</u>, not condemnation, i.e. works.

Mt.12:50 – Faith in the heavenly Father must be justified by <u>obeying His will</u>, i.e. works.

Mt.16:24-25 – Following Jesus [i.e. by Faith] includes <u>taking up the cross</u> after him, i.e. works.

Mt.22:34-40 – Following the "Law" [by Faith] is not enough, there must also be <u>love of neighbour</u>, i.e. works.

Mt.25:43-46 – There will be condemnation for those who did not <u>succour the thirsty, the hungry</u>, etc. i.e. works.

Mk.3:31-35 – Faith in God must be proved by <u>doing his will</u>, i.e. works.

Mk.12:28-34 – Faith in the Commandments [of the "Law"] is useless without <u>love of the neighbour</u>, i.e. works.

Mk.12:41-44 – Faith in God is shown by the <u>generosity</u> of the widow's mite, i.e. works.

Lk.6:27-38 – Faith must be proven by <u>blessing, compassion, love of enemies</u>, i.e. works.

Lk.6:46-49 – Faith in "the Lord" must be followed by <u>acts of obedience</u>, i.e. works.

Lk.9:23-26 – Following Jesus [by Faith] implies <u>renunciation, acceptance of the cross</u>, i.e. works.

Lk.11:23 – Being with Jesus means <u>gathering with him</u>, not scattering, i.e. works.

Lk.11:28 – Hearing the word of God [in Faith] means <u>keeping it</u>, i.e. works.

Lk.14:25-27 – <u>Total detachment</u> from earthly cares [by Faith] includes carrying one's cross, i.e. works.

Jn. 6:52-58 – Faith in Jesus means <u>taking his word literally</u>. Belief should result in works.

Jn.8:33, 57 – Faith in Abraham is not enough, one must believe in Jesus. Faith results in <u>repetition</u>, i.e. works.

Importance of St Paul

Paul gives us further penetrating insights into the discussion of **Faith** and **Works**. Being a Jew himself, a Pharisee trained at the school of Gamaliel (**Acts 22:3**), Paul knew intimately the Jewish Law [i.e. of Moses], and by his rejection of the same, clarifies the Church's teaching on these difficult subjects. Paul had been a very observant Jew, and was in the process of continuing persecution of the early Jewish-Christian Church when he was converted on the road to Damascus by a vision of Christ (**Acts 9:1-9; 22:4-16;**

26:12-23). He then passed three years in Arabia, meditating on the truth of the Christian message no doubt, and eventually spent the rest of his life travelling around the Mediterranean countries with the message of Jesus. He was finally beheaded in Rome by order of Nero. (See <u>Chap.15 – Peter and Paul</u>).

To understand Paul's teaching on Faith and Works, it is necessary to know something of Jewish Law.

There were, and still exist, 613 Commandments in Jewish Law which the practising Jew must obey. They deal with every single aspect of life – diet, clothing, eating, rest, work, travel, the Sabbath, sex, marriage, divorce, contracts, prayer, prohibitions, and so on. To be in the good books of "G_d", the faithful Jew had/has to scrupulously obey these Laws. Only those who had studied in the rabbinic schools would be able to know them all, or even to practise them. The ordinary people had to carry on with their lives, depending on the scribes, the doctors of the Law, and the Jewish hierarchy (Pharisees and Sadducees), to tell them what the Law demanded of them, and to tell them if or not they were in infraction of it. It is no wonder that Jesus lamented over the people, helpless like sheep (**<u>Jn.10:7-17</u>**)!

For his part, Paul taught that one is saved by Faith in Jesus Christ and His teaching, <u>not by obedience to the [Jewish] Law and its works</u>, i.e. by scrupulous obedience, e.g. the circumcision controversy, or the one on forbidden meats etc.

Some of Paul's teachings follow:

Rm. 1:17 – A man is justified by faith.
Rm.2:12 – 3:31 – Neither will the Law and its works, nor circumcision, nor even God's promises, can save the Jews, only Faith in Jesus.

Rm.4:13-25 – Abraham's faith is a model of Christian faith.

Rm.5:1-11 – Faith is the guarantee of salvation.

Rm.7:1-6 – The Christian is not bound by the Jewish Law and its prescriptions, i.e. obedience, meaning works.

Rm.13:8-10 – Love [i.e. practice by works] fulfils all the Commandments.

Gal.3:10-14 – Keeping of the [Jewish] Law brings a curse, but one is justified by faith in Christ.

Gal.3:23-29 – By faith in Christ, Christians are heirs to the promise (**Gal.4:31**), children of the freeborn wife [Sara].

Eph.2:10 – [Though] we are God's work of art, we must work for our salvation in fear and trembling, (**Phil.2:12-16**), [i.e. do not take God for granted through faith alone. One proves one's faith by producing fruit worthy of faith!]

Heb.10:1-10 – The sacrifices of the Law are useless; the sacrifice of Christ is the only one that counts.

Depending on the evidence of the aforesaid texts, the Church's teaching is clear. Faith in Christ is indeed necessary, taking into account those who refuse it by abysmal ignorance, and those who for one reason or another are unable to receive it. She teaches however that God's mercy extends even to those who are unable to be united by Baptism into the **Mystical Body of Christ**, the Church, and that they are in some way joined to the unfathomable depth of Christ's love, which cannot be denied. (See Chap.1 – The Divine Plan)

However, she also teaches that Faith must be accompanied by Works showing the beauty and justification of the Faith, that depending on one's faith alone is tantamount to taking God for granted. As Jesus himself said *"You must not put the Lord your God to the test"*. (**Dt.6:16; Lk.4:12**) – the belief that faith alone saves can lead to the grave sin of *presumption*. This would explain just why the Church, all through the centuries, has taken care to establish hospitals, orphanages, centres for the aged and infirm, schools, and a host of other works in favour of suffering humanity. Many countries, including those with Christian minorities, have benefited from this conviction that Jesus is alive and working through the many ministries of the Church. This conviction has been abundantly proved by the many saints who have laboured for Him in the light of faith, spreading the truth He brought into the world by their manifold works, many unto martyrdom.

Consider the many Orders, some of which have rescued prisoners, advanced Science and education, the great benefactors of children and youth.... consider Ignatius of Loyola, John of the Cross, Teresa of Avila, Augustine, Jerome, John Bosco, Damian of Molokai, Maximilian Kolbe, Ambrose, Edmund Campion, Vincent de Paul, Joan of Arc, Bede, Anthony of Padua, Thomas More, Maria Goretti, John Vianney, Monica, Gregory the Great, John-Paul ll, Francis of Assisi, Teresa of Kolkata, and the many thousands of others who fill the lists of saints and saintly persons in the history of the Church. They have abundantly spent themselves, not through fear, but through faith and love of their Lord and Saviour Jesus Christ.

NB: <u>The letters of Paul were written from around 50-65 AD, **before** any of the Gospels</u>, although Mark's is believed to have been published in 64 AD. Paul thought, spoke, and wrote like a converted Pharisee would. **This means that Paul had no idea of what the Church, under Peter and the others, taught about Faith and the necessity for Works under the new Christian dispensation to prove it**. As St James wrote: (**<u>Jas.2:17, 18, 20, 26</u>**) – Christian Faith without good works is useless, dead. [Luther had intended to remove this letter of James, along with others, from his translation of the Bible into German, but was persuaded to leave them in].

It has all been a labour of love, just love of Him and of their brothers and sisters, which fulfils the Commandments. Thus, Christian labour for suffering humanity necessarily involves expressions of this love, which are, plainly speaking, works of love.

However, a nagging question still remains and it is our duty to answer it. *What would Jesus himself say to the thesis of Luther, that faith alone suffices?* Jesus himself will reply to this - he never backed down from a fight! We observe:

'Hearing' and 'listening' are not the same thing. A child hears his mother's correction, but when she says ***"Listen to me!"***, he is obliged to ***do*** what she orders, otherwise it's trouble! It is the same with the words of Jesus, who often uses "action words" e.g. keep or keeps, does, acts, or make, as in the following Gospel examples, which often repeat themselves.

These words call for a commitment by the hearer, a putting into action, an actualisation of the words spoken, which are not meant to be merely heard, but listened to and acted upon Thus:

<u>Mt.5:19</u> – "[He] who ***keeps*** [the commandments] and ***teaches*** them will be considered great in the kingdom of heaven".

<u>Lk.2:49</u> – "Did you not know that ***I must be busy*** with my Father's affairs?" [At 12 years, a knowledge of action to come]

<u>Lk.6:46-49</u> – "Why do you call me, 'Lord, Lord', and not ***do*** what I say? He who listens to my word and ***acts*** on them ....[builds on rock]. But he who listens and ***does nothing......*** [builds on sand]......".

<u>Lk.9:23</u> – ["Let any follower] of mine ***renounc***e himself and ***take up his cross*** daily......". [Other "action words"]

<u>Jn.8:31</u> – "If you ***make*** my word your home, you will indeed be my disciples". [i.e. action according to the words].

Jn.8:51 – "Whoever *keeps* my word will never see death".

Jn.9:4 – "I must *carry out the work* of the one who sent me". [More action words – cf. **Lk.2:49** above]

Jn.12:47 – "If anyone <u>hears</u> my words and <u>does not keep them</u> faithfully......" [Non-action]

:48 – "He who <u>rejects</u> me <u>and refuses</u> my words has his judge already". [Non-action].

:49 – "For what I have spoken does not come from myself...... what *I had to speak* was <u>commanded by the Father</u> who sent me". [Jesus' obedience to the word of the Father, the example he gives to us].

Jn.14:21 – "Anyone who receives my commandments and *keeps* them will be one who loves me...."

:23 - "If anyone loves me he will *keep* my word".........

:24 – "Those who do not love me *do not keep* my words....."

Jn.15:10 – "If you *keep* my commandments you will remain in my love, as I have *kept* my Father's commandments and remain in his love".

Jn.15:14 – "You are my friends, if you *do* what I command you".

Jn.15:20 – [The hostile world]...... "If they *kep*t my word, they will *keep yours* as well..."

:22 – "They have no excuse for their sin".

To clinch his teaching, Jesus uses a little parable to show that <u>***actions because of faith***</u> speak louder than words.

Mt.7:21 – "It is not those who say to me, 'Lord, Lord', who will enter the kingdom of heaven, but the person who ***does*** **:24-27** *the will* of my Father in heaven"...... He who listens to these words of mine and ***acts*** on them....[will have built his house on rock. The one who doesn't will have built on sand]. (cf. <u>Chap.16 - The Rock</u>, and **Lk.6:46-49**, above).

Considering all the above, it is clear that Faith is important in the life of every believer. That it can be asked for in prayer is a truth of the Catholic Church from the beginning. However, to believe that Faith alone saves, and ***to presume*** that one is saved through *Faith alone*, howsoever one may have sinned, is to sin by **Presumption**, one of the main subjects of contention between Catholics and the heirs of the Reformation. (See Chap.12 – The Reformation, Luther's Teaching)

To believe that forgiveness is received by faith alone is to reject the words of Jesus himself in **Jn.20:19-23**, when he delegated to the Apostles the privilege of forgiving sins, the Sacrament of Reconciliation. Believing that merely asking God for forgiveness, and to have received it in this way, is to forgive oneself, to justify oneself, not to receive the real pardon He offers through Jesus. (See Chap.3 – The WORD).

Therefore, it is not surprising when a Separated Brother, [having rejected these words of Jesus], not having anyone to forgive his sins except by asking God for forgiveness -which he believes is accorded - is in fact forgiving himself, which is a form of auto-justification. This leads to **Presumption**, the belief of being saved by faith alone. A judge in a court cannot forgive himself for a speeding charge, nor can a Catholic priest forgive himself of his own sins by presumption.

A Separated Brother in many cases may be unsure that his sins are forgiven, and so he may go to his Pastor, who may tell him that he is forgiven, but as the Pastor himself is not a priest, the unsure Brother finds himself going to his psychiatrist or psychologist, to remove his ill feelings, his depression, his unsureness. Which may help, but wouldn't it be easier to follow the words of Jesus and go to a priest? And thereby hangs a tale…

God is omnipotent, a God of Reason (***Logos***), yet his Divinity is limited by his own Being, his laws of logic and natural law, his absolute character of Reasonableness. Thus, he cannot, unless by a Divine act of redefining himself and his own Divinity, which is inherently impossible to him, contradict his own Divinity and Omnipotence. He cannot decide that 1 and 1 can also be 3, or that a square can also be a circle, that "up" can also be "down" at the same time, etc. etc.

In the same way, God is also limited by man's use or mis-use of his God-given Free Will, which any believer can use to put into action his faith, to access the graces he needs by obeying the words of Jesus, as shown above. It is through Free Will that one keeps, acts, or performs the actions necessary to be worthy of Christ himself, so as to one day enter into the Presence of the Almighty. It is also through its mis-use that man falls into sin, the denial of God's will.

Thus, Predestination, the Arbitrariness of God, and the lack of Free Will, all of which are believed in and taught by several sects of the Separated Brethren, and above all by Islam, have no place in the Catholic Church. Which is why Our Lord had promised to send the Holy Spirit, to protect us, and to show the truth about Sin and Judgement (**Jn.16:8-11**).

If you remain constant in your faith in the face of trial, the Lord will give you peace and rest for a time in this world, and forever in the next. (St Jerome Emiliani)

-o-o-o-o-o-o-o-

CHAPTER 15
Peter and Paul

Their Importance

It is indeed "meet and just" to consider in detail these two giants of the Catholic Church, not only because each has contributed immensely to its growth and cohesion, but also to its understanding of God's plan for humanity, its theology. Thousands of books in many languages have been written about each, but this brief article only wishes to portray the elements which each has contributed to mankind, particularly in the case of St Paul.

Many non-Catholic Christians have even surmised that Paul was the real founder of the Church, thereby downplaying the importance of Peter, chosen by Jesus himself to be the Rock in **Mt.16:13-20**, from whom the historical and chronological proofs of the Papacy derive. It is therefore necessary to understand more deeply the different characteristics of each of our subjects.

We know little about Simon, surnamed Peter, about his family, his children, his origins. He and his brother Andrew must have owned a boat, for they were fishermen in Capernaum, a fishing village on the west side of the lake of Galilee. They were called by Jesus to follow him, to become "fishers of men", and they did so at once, leaving their nets (**Mt.4:18-22**). Peter had a mother-in-law who served Jesus and his followers in Peter's home, having been cured of a fever by Jesus (**Mt.8:14-15**). It is not clear why Peter's wife is not mentioned; thus, it may be surmised that she had died. An apocryphal document refers to a daughter Elizabeth with him in Rome, but other than this person, nothing more is said about his family.

Peter says little in the Gospels, perhaps he was the taciturn type, trying to understand just who Jesus was. His faith seemed solid, and for having recognised Jesus as "the Christ", he is chosen to be the Rock (see Chap.16 – The Rock), but shortly afterwards is severely reproached by Jesus, who calls him *"Satan!"*, for having contradicted Jesus' prophecy that he must be put to death and afterwards rise again (**Mt.16:21-23**). Later on, when surprisingly Jesus comes walking on the water, he impetuously asks Jesus to let him come to him. He jumps into the water, begins to walk upon it, takes fright and begins to sink. He cries out in fear *"Lord, save me!"*, which Jesus did, reproaching him gently for his lack of faith (**Mt.14:22-33**).

Peter and two others were present at the Transfiguration, and there again his impetuosity is clearly shown (**Mt. 17:1-8**). This flaw in his character is shown by his brazen affirmation that he would never betray Jesus *"even if I have to die with you"* (**Mt. 26:30-35**), and even more so when he denies Jesus three times, at the time of Jesus' trial before the Sanhedrin (**Mt. 26:69-75**; **Mk.14:66-72**; **Lk.22:54-62**; **Jn.18:15-27**), thereby fulfilling Jesus' prophecy that he would deny him.

Notwithstanding these weaknesses in Peter's character, Jesus chose to reconfirm Peter as the leader of the group, doing so in **Jn.21:15-19**. After the Ascension, Peter went to Rome to evangelise, where tradition tells us that he was crucified.

Being only a simple uneducated fisherman (**Acts 4:13**) Peter would not have had much to do with the Jewish hierarchy and its doings in Jerusalem. For him the synagogue at Capernaum sufficed, the rabbi there would have had all the answers. He would not have had much knowledge about the Law of Moses, he just followed the teachings given to the common people. But he came to understand who Jesus really was after the Resurrection, and spoke to the crowd about this in his first effort after the coming of the Holy Spirit at Pentecost (**Acts 2:1-41**; **3:1-26**; **4:1-22**), and he even faced bravely the Sanhedrin, saying *"Obedience to God comes before obedience to men!"* (**Acts 4:19-20; 5:29-33**), when he and others had been arrested.

Before ascending to the Father, Jesus had commanded the Apostles to *"Go and teach the nations, baptising them in the Name of the Father, of the Son, and of the Holy Spirit"* (**Mt.28:18-20**). However, entry into the early Church was most probably by baptism "in the name of Jesus-Christ", seen in **Acts 2:37-41** and **10:48**, by Peter, **8:38** by Philip, **9:18** by Ananias, **16:15, 34**, and **19:5** by Paul. No doubt the Trinitarian formula of baptism had not yet been fully understood and put into effect, so the simpler form was used. Some of those baptised had previously been baptised into the "baptism of John", but that being only "one of repentance", were re-baptised "in the name of Jesus-Christ" (**Acts 19:5**).

Peter then goes north with the Good News, cures a paralytic at Lydda (**Acts 9:32-35**), raises a dead woman to life (**Acts 9:36-42**), visits a pagan Roman centurion and converts his family (**Acts 10:1-48**), justifies his conduct before the other Apostles at Jerusalem (**Acts 11:1-18**), is arrested and imprisoned by Herod's order, is freed miraculously (**Acts 12:1-19**).

Later on, at Antioch in Syria he was reproached by Paul for having eaten with Jews, through human respect for the pagans (**Gal.2:11-14**). He later travels to Rome, and Nero orders his death. Thus far for Jesus' Peter, the "Fisher of men".

Peter wrote two letters, no doubt helped by his companion Silvanus, a speaker of good Greek (**1Pet.5:12**). Both letters give a comprehensive account of the life of the newly-baptised Christians. Briefly, he refers to salvation through the sufferings and Resurrection of Jesus, who has fulfilled the prophecies. Christians are all called to a sanctifying love, being a nation of priests. He also teaches about relationships to unbelievers, between masters and slaves, about marriage, the suffering they may have to undergo, but Christ will return surely. As leader, he gives advice on clean Christian living, stressing that prophecies are from God, and that they must beware of false teachers, because there will indeed be a punishment.

Then in his second letter (**2Pet.3:15-16**) he refers to Paul, saying *"**Some points of Paul's letters are hard to understand**"*.

ooooooooooooooooooo

This phrase of Peter, with the careful research of biblical scholars, lead us to understand that the letters of Paul, who had never met the living Jesus, were written ***before*** the Gospels. He was born as Saul of Jewish parents of the tribe of Benjamin in Tarsus (Turkey), educated in Jerusalem as a Pharisee under the great Gamaliel (**Acts 22:3**; **Acts 5:34-40** – showing that both Paul and Gamaliel were alive at that time). Being a Pharisee, Saul [a.k.a. Paul] was highly educated in the Mosaic Law, and began to persecute the early Church, considering it a heresy (**Acts 8:3**; **9:1-2**; **26:9-11**). He was converted by a vision of Jesus on his way to Damascus to capture early Christians (**Acts 9:3-25**; **26:12-18**). He spent some time in Arabia after this (**Gal.1:17**), returned to Damascus, and then went to Jerusalem after three years (**Gal.1:18**). He was feared by the Apostles because of his reputation, but after his presentation by Barnabas (**Acts 9:26-30**) and acceptance by the Apostles, he left to visit the early communities in Syria and Cilicia (**Gal.1:22-23**), spending fourteen years there before returning to Jerusalem (**Gal.2:1**). Then he began his journeys to the pagan countries to the north-west, Greece, Turkey, Macedonia.

Given the difficult means of travel and communication then existing, it is frankly amazing that Paul – whose name had been changed from Saul – was able to make three missionary voyages by boat across the dangerous Mediterranean to found new communities of Christians, returning always to Jerusalem to report. **He worked from around 50 AD to 65 AD**. The new communities received letters of encouragement and/or reproach, nine in all – to the Thessalonians (2) from 50-51, to the Corinthians (2) in 57, to the Galatians and Romans in 57 and 58, to the Philippians in 56 and 57, to the Ephesians and Colossians in 61 and 63. Paul also wrote to three individuals – to Philemon (61 or 63), to Timothy (2) and to Titus, around 65, and was then taken to Rome and was imprisoned. Tradition tells us that he was finally beheaded by order of Nero.

As reported above, Paul did not have the benefit of the Gospels for information about the details of the Jesus story, his letters were all written *before* the Gospels. The earliest Gospel, that of Mark, came out only in 64 AD, those of Matthew and Luke, including Acts, coming out between 70-80 AD. John's, the last, saw the light around 90, becoming well known in the early Church before 150. Perhaps the Apostles did not hurry to write the story of Jesus, believing that the Master would be returning in a short while.

It seems to be clear that Paul would not have known about the Trinitarian formula for Baptism as anteriorly commanded by Jesus, and so the simplest form, "in the name of Jesus-Christ", (the One who had turned his life completely around) was used., St Luke, the companion of his voyages, records his efforts in **Acts 16:15, 34**, and **19:5**.

Paul therefore wrote as an educated convert would, giving a lot of practical advice about living a proper Christian life, leaving aside worldly temptations, reproaching severely sins and various impurities of the flesh. In **1Cor.11:23-30** he gives a masterly exposition of the Last Supper, warning of its consequences those who receive unworthily.

However, as a former Pharisee and student of Pharisees, he has two particular preoccupations. His first is faith in the salvation brought by Jesus, the Messiah who has fulfilled the prophecies, who by his cross and resurrection has given new hope to those who had none (**1Cor.15:1-58**).

His second preoccupation is the abrogation of the Law of Moses by Jesus, who has rendered it useless (**Eph.2:14-17**), including its observation, considered works, for the person to be considered righteous. He says *"What makes a man righteous is not obedience to the Law, but faith in Jesus Christ"* (**Gal.2:16**), and *"If the Law can justify us, there is no point in the death of Christ"* (**Gal.2:21**), among many other references.

Writing *before* the Gospels came out, Paul had no idea of what the Apostles thought of faith and the necessity to prove it, as in (**James 2:14-26**), *"Faith is like that: if good works do not go with it, it is quite dead.....Do realise, you senseless man, that faith without good deeds is useless....A body dies when it is* *separated from the spirit, and in the same way faith is dead if it is separated from good deeds".*

Luther had got it all wrong, mixing up the rejection of works of the Law of Moses with the necessary works of the new Christian dispensation, misunderstanding the teaching of the Apostles. (See Chap.14 – Sola Fide).

If ***"Paul is hard to understand"!*** as Peter had written, it is no wonder that Martin Luther, considering Paul's letter 1500 years later, would find it even more difficult to understand Paul's theology, having studied this scholarly discipline for only 18 months!
(See Chap.12 – The Reformation).

-o-o-o-o-o-o-o-

>Come and listen, all you who fear God,
>While I tell you what he has done for me;
>When I uttered my cry to him
>And high praise was on my tongue,
>Had I been guilty in my heart,
>The Lord would never have heard me.
>But God not only heard me,
>He listened to my prayer.
>Blessed be God
>Who neither ignored my prayer,
>Nor deprived me of his love.
>
>(Ps.66(65), vs. 16-20)

-o-o-o-o-o-o-o-

CHAPTER **16**

the Rock

The "Rock" – Catholicism Justified

<u>Mt.16:13-20</u> – When Jesus came to the region of Caesarea Philippi, he put this question to his disciples, ***"Who do people say the Son of Man is?"*** And they said, "Some say he is John the Baptist, some Elijah, others Jeremiah or one of the prophets". ***"But you"***, he said, ***"Who do you say I am?"*** Then Simon [Peter] spoke up, "You are the Christ", he said, "the Son of the living God". Jesus replied, ***"<u>Simon, son of Jonah, you are a happy man!</u> Because it was not flesh and blood that revealed this to you, but my Father in heaven. So, I now say to you<u>: you are Peter, and on this rock,</u> I will build my Church. And the gates of the underworld can never hold out against it. I will give you the keys of the kingdom of heaven: whatever you bind on earth shall be considered bound in heaven; whatever you loose on earth shall be considered loosed in heaven"***. Then he gave his disciples strict orders not to tell anyone that he was the Christ.

The giving – or changing – of someone's name, as in Baptism, or to nuns, monks, or priests in religious Orders when taking their final vows, or to Jews on circumcision, is an important event in the life of each recipient. Following are three Jewish personalities with important links in holy history. In each case it is clear that Yahweh-God had occasioned the change, and in each case, there will be an extra important role for the person to fulfil.

1) **Gen. 17:1-14** – Abram's name is changed to Abraham. His role:

   - he will be father to a multitude of nations
   - kings will issue from him
   - he is party to a perpetual Covenant with God
   - all Canaan will be given to him, in perpetuity
   - Yahweh will be his/their God
   - the Covenant will be maintained to all generations
   - Circumcision of male children will be the sign of the Covenant

Conclusion – Abraham's tribal nature is enlarged to universal dimensions. His descendants will live in a perpetual Covenant with a unique God, with circumcision as a sign of its trustworthiness. This will be extended to his son Isaac.

2) **Gen.17:15-17** – Abraham's wife's name, Sarai, is changed to Sara – nations and kings will come from her. Her role:

   - she will be the mother of the son of the promise, Isaac
   - her son Isaac will receive a Covenant in perpetuity
   - Yahweh will be the God of Isaac and his descendants.

Conclusion – The Covenant in favour of the son of Abraham ("son of the promise") will be fulfilled, because of her.

3) **Gen.32:26-32** – Story of Isaac's son Jacob, who had tricked his brother Esau to give up his birthright.

v.29 – Isaac's son Jacob's name is changed to Israel. His role as revealed:
- Israel will find strength in God
- Israel will prevail against men.

Conclusion – Israel will prevail against men, because of God's protection.

In **Mt.16:13-20**, Simon bar Jonah's name was changed to Peter [Petros= rock, in Greek] by Jesus himself. Jesus arrogates to himself the right of Almighty God to change the name of an important person in holy history, and in doing so, implicitly claims divine right to do so, i.e. this is one more claim among many that Jesus makes to be God himself!

But, what does this word "rock" mean? Why did Jesus choose it to apply it to a single person, and why is Simon the only one in the entire Bible to bear such an odd name? What would be his role, and what would be the conclusion, as above? The Bible has many references to the word "rock", found particularly as synonymous with Almighty God Himself. There are many indeed, but here are some of the most evident:

Dt.32:3b,4 – Oh, tell the greatness of our God! He is the Rock; his work is perfect, for all his ways are equity.

Dt.32:15 – [Jacob] disowned the God who made him, dishonoured the Rock, his salvation.

Dt.32:18 – You forgot the Rock who begot you, unmindful now of the God who fathered you.

Dt.32:30 – How could two put ten thousand to flight, were it not that their Rock has sold them?

Dt.32:31 - But their rock is not like our Rock, our enemies are no intercessors.

2Sam.22:32 – Who else is God but Yahweh, who else a Rock but out God?

2Sam.22:47 – Life to Yahweh! Blessed be my Rock! Exalted be the God of my salvation.

2Sam.23:3 – The God of Jacob has spoken, the Rock of Israel has said to me…..

Is.26:4 – Trust in Yahweh forever, for Yahweh is the everlasting Rock.

Ps.18:2a,2c – Yahweh is my Rock and my bastion….I take shelter in him, my Rock, my shield…..

Ps.18:31 – Who else is God but Yahweh, who else a Rock but our God?

Ps.18:46 – Life to Yahweh! Blessed be my Rock! Exalted be the God of my salvation….

Ps.19:14 – May the words of my mouth find favour in your presence, Yahweh, my Rock, my Redeemer!

Ps.28:1 – I cry to you, Yahweh, my Rock! Do not be deaf to me, or…… I shall go down to the Pit….

Ps.31:2,3 – Be a sheltering Rock for me…. For you are my Rock, my fortress…… guide me, lead me!

Ps.42-43:9 – Let me say to God, my Rock, "Why do you forget me?.....oppressed by the enemy?"

Ps.62:7 – Rest in God, my safety, my glory, the Rock of my strength.

Ps.71:3a,3c – Be a sheltering Rock for me…. For you are my Rock, my fortress…

Ps.73:26 – My flesh and heart pine with love, my heart's Rock, my own, God for ever!

Ps.78:35 – They came to their senses, remembering that God was their Rock, God the most high, their redeemer.

Ps.89:26 – He will invoke me, 'My father, my God and Rock of my safety', and I shall make him my first-born, the Most High for kings on earth. I will keep my love for him always; my covenant with him will stand.

Ps.144:1 – Blessed be Yahweh, my Rock, who trains my hands for war, and my fingers for battle……

1Cor.10:1-4, St. Paul says: *"Our fathers….. all drank the same spiritual drink, since they all drank from the spiritual rock that followed them as they went, and that Rock was Christ"*. Paul's faith in Jesus is evident!

In the secular context, "rock" means solidity, immovability, strength, trustworthiness, something on which one has absolute confidence, which gives meaning to life, a security, a solid foundation for building something upon it.

But biblically, it is applied to *someone*. All these qualities are applied to Yahweh-God, who Himself, through Jesus his Son, is therefore the Truth which does not, and cannot, deceive. Jesus identifies himself with this term "Rock", as "I", Son of the living God, the Yahweh of the Jewish people, when he says **"I am the Way, the Truth, and the Life"** (**Jn.14:6**).

Jesus therefore is himself the Rock to which all the aforementioned texts apply, and in the text of **Mt.16 (above)**, he is in fact ***delegating*** the trustworthiness of God himself to a fallible human being, Simon, who is to be the Rock of the Church, the only Church intended by Christ. This is the only known biblical case of delegated *substantial (being-ness)* identity.

Briefly, Peter's role(s) would be:

- the solid foundation of a singular spiritual entity founded by Jesus, which is the Church.
- he is responsible for this Church.
- he has received a delegation of authority from Christ himself.
- his authority will be exercised with the backing of Christ himself.
- Evil will never overcome the Church, guaranteed by Christ himself.

Conclusion – Peter's authority would extend to the Church founded by Christ, which was called "Catholic", [universal] for the first time around AD 107 by St Ignatius of Antioch, in a letter to the Christians of Smyrna while on his way to Rome, to his eventual martyrdom in the Colosseum arena.

Indeed, Jesus chose Simon-Peter to be his Representative on Earth, not any of the *seven "reformers" (cf. below) to do this holy work. There may be fallings-away, unfaithfulness, unworthiness, all part of the human condition, but Jesus took the risk of confiding his *One* Church to unworthy people, mindful of their weaknesses. One can only marvel at the boldness of making such an unimaginable choice! The Rock chose a mere human to be the "Petros", Rock, which would be the very *substantial (being-ness)* nature of the Church founded by Jesus.

Although Simon-Peter had denied Jesus three times before the condemnation and crucifixion of his Master (**Jn.18:17-18, 25-27**), yet Jesus, after the Resurrection, chose to re-confirm this choice of Simon-Peter three times (**Jn.21:15-17**), thereby affirming that His Vicar on earth would have the supreme charge of feeding and caring for the "sheep" of the Lord. One would be supremely foolish to deny Jesus' intention of <u>leaving a visible Church on earth, built on rock,</u> with authority guaranteed by Him, not merely one composed of an amorphous and incoherent mass of believers (**Mt.7:21-27**).

Jesus also self-identifies as being intimately familiar with the Yahweh of the Jewish people, changing the awesome nomenclature *["I AM WHO AM"]* (**Ex.3:13-15**), to the familiar "Abba" [Papa] used by the Jewish children of today to a beloved parent, and in Gethsemane puts himself completely at the disposal of his Abba: – ***"Abba, take this cup away from me. But let it be as you, not I, would have it"***, knowing beforehand the terrible sufferings he would soon have to undergo, (**Mk.14:36**).

To the Jews who wish to stone him, who say: *"We are not stoning you for doing a good work, but for blasphemy: you are only a man, and you claim to be God!"*(**Jn.10:33**); he had said: ***"The Father and I are one"*** (**Jn.10:30**), and ***"You will know for sure, that the Father is in me, and I am in the Father"*** (**Jn.10:38**). To the Jews who indignantly say: *"You are not yet fifty, and you have seen Abraham?"*, he replies ***"I tell you most solemnly, before Abraham ever was, I AM!"***. He clearly claims divinity using the Tetragrammaton name of Yahweh *["I AM WHO AM"]*, which had been revealed to Moses (**Ex.3:14**), and which in Jesus' time was used only by the High Priest (**Jn.8:57-58**) for the Temple sacrifices.

He thus identifies himself totally with the Father in these and in many other contexts, e.g. (**Mk.14:62-63**) – The High Priest asked him: *"Are you the Christ, the Son of the Blessed One?"*. *"I AM"*, said Jesus, ***"and you will see the Son of Man seated at the*** *right hand of the Power and coming with the clouds of heaven"* (**Dan.7:11-14**) – the title "Son of Man" was understood by the Jewish hierarchy to refer to someone of divine origin. The *"I AM"* Jesus used was clearly a blasphemy for the High Priest, who tore his robes, as custom demanded (**Mk.14:63**).

Jesus also identifies himself fully with the Church he had founded on Simon-Peter, which had to undergo much opposition. After the Resurrection and Ascension of Our Lord, when the early Church was gathering many adepts, a certain Pharisee named Saul, who had never known Jesus, was on his way to Damascus to seek out and arrest those who followed the "Way", when a light from heaven made him fall to the ground. Then he heard a voice saying: *"Saul, Saul, why are you persecuting me?"*. *"Who are you, Lord?"*, he asked. *"I am Jesus, and you are persecuting me"!* said the voice, (**Acts 9:2-6**). Saul later became (St.) Paul, and it is clear here that Jesus is identifying himself with the very Church he had founded on Simon-Peter, the *"me"* said twice referring expressly to the Church Saul was persecuting.

From its very beginnings to this day the Church has always understood and taught that She and Jesus form an unique body, to which there is no parallel. It is not the same as the union of a physical body, nor that of a business corporation, (**1Cor. 12:12-30**; **Eph.1:22-23, 4:13** etc.). [See Chap.1 "The Divine Plan").

Pius XII defined this as a dogma of faith of the Catholic Church in 1943 in his encyclical *"Mystici Corporis Christi"* :

[the **Mystical Body of Christ**], *to which all baptised members of the Catholic Church belong, and to which all other properly baptised Christians also belong, though imperfectly, not having been able to preserve unity or communion under the successor of Peter through separations for which, often enough, men of both sides were to blame.*

Many brethren remain separated, though not necessarily through their own fault. (Vatican ll, *"Unitatis Reintegratio"* [Decree on Ecumenism]; Catechism of the Catholic Church, 'Profession of Faith', No.838).

The present Ecumenical Movement is trying to restore the unity broken by the Western Schism (1054) and the Reformation of the 16th century. It is to be earnestly hoped that the unity lost in past centuries may one day be restored. This should be the constant prayer of those who cherish the name of Jesus, Saviour and Redeemer, for ***"On this Rock I will build My Church"***.

The Church therefore is built on Christ Himself, the immovable and trustworthy Rock, with Peter as its Head on earth.

-o-o-o-o-o-o-o-

<u>Names of the foremost Reformers</u>:

*Luther; *Melanchthon; *Calvin; *Bucer; *Zwingli; *Knox; *Henry Vlll. (See <u>Chap.12 – The Reformation</u>)

-o-o-o-o-o-o-o-

> Bring us back, God our Saviour,
> Master your resentment against us.
> Do you mean to be angry with us for ever,
> To prolong your wrath age after age?
> Will you not give us life again,
> For your people to rejoice in you?
> Yahweh, show us your love,
> Grant us your saving help.
>
> Love and Loyalty now meet,

Righteousness and Peace now embrace;
Loyalty reaches up from earth
And Righteousness leans down from heaven.

(Ps.85(84), vs.4-7,10-11).

-o-o-o-o-o-o-o-

CHAPTER 17
Feminine Element

Necessity of the Feminine Element in Religion

In studies of all known societies, the male element – the man – seems to have always held the preponderant role. The man is the hunter, the builder of the family house, whatever form this may take, whether of adobe mud, logs and wattle, stone, brick, glass, etc. The woman of the family has usually been the drawer of water, gatherer of the fire-wood for cooking, cleaner of the house, bearer and carer of children, the one always with a secondary role. The man normally makes decisions for the family's good, its moving around, and the same goes for the decisions concerning village concerns. Rarely does the woman have an important voice in these decisions; she is traditionally kept in a submissive state, although there are indeed societies which have taken women more seriously, and have indeed accepted that their voice at times can be important.

In ancient religions, male gods seem to have also been more to the fore. We know of the <u>ancient **Greek** ones</u>, with their manly attributes – Zeus (King), Poseidon (Sea), Ares (War), Apollo (Sun), Hermes (Messenger), Dionysus (Wine), Hephaestus (Blacksmith), and Hades (Underworld), while the female ones are mainly relegated to relationships – Hera (Queen), Demeter (Fertility), Athena (Wisdom), Aphrodite (Love), Hestia (Hearth), with the exception of Artemis, (Hunt).

With few exceptions, the ancient gods of **Rome** followed those of Greece, the manly pursuits being arrogated to the male ones – Jupiter (King), Janus (Gates), Mercury (Commerce), Neptune (Sea), Saturn (Time), Mars (War), Bacchus (Wine), Vulcan (Blacksmith), and Pluto (Underworld), while the females had once more mainly the roles of keepers of relationships – Fortuna (Luck), Venus (Love), Vesta (Hearth), Victoria (Victory), Juno (Marriage), and Diana (Moon, Hunt).

The gods of **India**, the males – Brahma (Heavens), Vishnu (Underworld), Skanda (War), Surya (Sun), Maheshwar (Seas), and the females – Durga (Solace), Kali (Sex, War), Lakshmi (Purity), Saraswathi (Arts), and those of ancient **Egypt**, the males – Amun-Ra (King, Sun), Anubis (Dead), Horus (Sky), Osiris (Underworld), Ptah (Craftsmen), Seth (Chaos), and the females – Hathor (Beauty, Music), Isis (Life), Nut (Sky-dome) – have more or less closely followed the essential necessities of every society, each fulfilling a role in the understanding of their societies which, in the absence of a revealed religion, were most important in holding these societies together, delineating their structures and giving importance to the various levels of authority, occupations, crafts, and guilds, which gave sense to them. In the first century AD Catholic-Christianity arrived in **India** with Saints Thomas and Matthew, in the district of Kerala. Many Christian communities live there today, but most of India still believes in its polytheistic pantheon of divinities and "avatars", the attributes of divinities.

Apart from a large group of local deities, gods, goddesses, and spirits believed in and worshipped by pre-Islamic **Arabia** – among them Atarsamain, Nukhay, Ruldalu, Orotait, Urania, Sin – which had their steles and plaques among the 365 others in the cubic Kaaba building in Makkah, the pre-eminent gods were Al-ilah (Moon)), Hubal (Chief), and the goddesses Al-Lat (Beauty), Al-Uzza (Fertility), and Manat (Destiny), considered to be daughters of Hubal. Lesser influences in Arabia came from Judaism (the Diaspora Jews), Zoroastrianism (from Iran), heretical Christians (Nestorians), and Hinduism, from the neighbouring nations of Greece, Rome, Iran, and India. It is believed that certain Arabian gods, male and female, were influenced by the proximity of these countries. [It is also believed that the Kaaba was a trading outpost of the former Indian kingdom of Chandra-Gupta, but investigation into this is prohibited]

The ancient kingdoms of **Mexico**, particularly those of the Aztecs, also had their pantheon of over 200 male and female gods and goddesses, each with his or her special role and importance in their societies, e.g. gods of War, Sun, Night, Water, Healing, Fertility, etc etc, as in the gods of other countries. As in all pre-Christian societies, gods of both sexes were absolutely essential for giving sense to their existence, their lives and their futures.

In all the above regions and their religions, although male gods were considered to be the most important, echoing male importance in human society, yet there was a certain importance given to female goddesses, as proponents of relationships, fertility, beauty, etc. However, there was nothing like equality in these relationships. Differences were still important.

With the arrival of Catholic Christianity, *post* 33 AD (the Ascension of Jesus) – the fulfilment of the revealed religion of the Jewish people - the gods and goddesses of **Greece**, **Rome** and **Egypt** were eventually replaced by belief in the Holy Trinity - three Divine Persons in One God, with Jesus as Redeemer, the Second Person of the Trinity. He is the God-man in whom Christians believe, a unique Being possessed of two natures, divine and human (Council of Chalcedon, 451 AD).

Islam began in Arabia on the death of Muhammad (632 AD). Hubal and the 365 divinities in the Kaaba were eliminated, Al-ilah became the chief god Allah, and following the conquests of the Islamic hordes, most of the Christians in Egypt, except for small resistant communities, were forcibly converted to Islam, as were the Christians in North Africa. For the past almost 1400 years Islam has waged *jihad* wars against Europe and India, forcing many of these peoples into attitudes of defence and retaliation to protect their beliefs, all of which have soured relationships between other nations and Islam.

This religion, which in fact is a political ideology couched in religious terminology, is altogether of a different category. Apart from four women considered "perfect" in Islam – Muhammad's wife Khadijah, his daughter Fatima, the wife of Pharaoh, and Mary, mother of Issa (Jesus) - there is no outstanding female element in Islam, in fact there is no feminine element either in the nature of Allah. The Qur'an's Allah is force, violence, instigator of *jihad,* killing of apostates, stoning of adulterers, murder of infidels, etc. There is nothing feminine about Allah, - his nature is pure Will, i.e. it has no purpose other than its own exercise, totally arbitrary and without reason and direction. Muslims are obliged to follow this Will, howsoever contradictory it may seem. Divorce is possible only by men, there is polygamy, marriages to children, temporary marriages, etc. Because of this preponderance of masculinity in Islam, there are ingrown attitudes of aggression, arbitrariness, lack of pardon, imposition of the will, fanaticism, degradation of womanhood, and to this day there are very few examples of women being considered equal to men. Although certain Islamic countries have allowed minimal rights to women, e.g. permission to drive a car, this is certainly not universal in Islam. There is still a long way to go to....

Judaism is the only other religion which firmly believes only in what can be termed a "male" God, now known as Ha-Shem (the Name), whereas "he" was formerly known as Yahweh (from YHWH in **Ex. 3:13-15**). In fact, <u>Ha-Shem has both male and female characteristics</u>, male because "he" is God of armies (Sabaoth, e.g. in Joshua's conquest of the Promised Land), and female because of the care "she" takes of the Chosen People through the centuries, and how in Leviticus "she" regulates in a feminine fashion the wearing of the priests' clothing, the decoration of the altars, health, sexuality, impurities, the way they should act and react with others, etc. "He" or "She" is thus technically neutral, a male-female symbiotic union.

One of the essential differences between these two outlooks on faith and God, Islam and Christianity, is that, contrary to Islam, which believes only in a Uni-Personal male god, Allah, Trinitarian Christians hold great respect for women and their uniqueness, offering possibilities unknown to males. Traditional Christianity honours women like no other faith, which is evident in all countries where this faith has been introduced. This has come about through the gradual development through the centuries of Mariology, the theological studies of the role and importance of the Virgin Mary, as indicated by her official titles in the Catholic Church. These follow here:

The Five Marian Dogmas of the Church

1) The Virgin birth – (Cncl. 1st of Nicaea 325 AD)

2) The Perpetual Virginity of Mary – (Cncl. of Constantinople 533 AD)- ("**Aeiparthenos**"- Ever Virgin)

3) Mother of God (Cncl. of Ephesus 431AD – **Theotokos**).

4) Immaculate Conception – (Pius lX in 1854 AD)

5) Assumption of Mary – (Pius Xll in 1950 AD)

Through the social application of the first three of these Dogmas, the Age of Chivalry in the Middle Ages, the respect for women, became a prime mover for Catholic-Christian peoples, and many beautiful cathedrals and churches in Europe and elsewhere have been built and dedicated in honour of the Virgin, e.g. Notre Dame and Chartres in France, around the European world – and in the USA, Germany, Italy, India, Russia, even in Africa and Antarctica!

When king John of England signed the Magna Carta by 1215, current despotism began to decline. According to historians of law, this was "the greatest constitutional document of all time". With the opening-up of the possibility of public approval of laws by voting and representation, despotism gradually ended in countries where the Faith had entered, and has influenced the Constitutions of many countries, helping to install democratic principles. This gave women the possibility of seeking further involvement in public life of all nations where democracy was established, helped by the deep respect felt for the Virgin Mary and the Mariological theology which resulted.

This has resulted in emancipation for women in these countries. They have been granted by Civil Law the right to vote (sometimes with great opposition from men!), the right to sue for divorce, to choose their life's partner, to have a University education, to present themselves for elections, to protest against injustices in society, to engage in sporting activities, to demand fair treatment in marriages, etc. etc. This in great measure has been the reason for the installation of democracy in countries influenced by

Christianity, evidenced by the importance that women now play in the political spheres of European and American countries. Even India, still with its plethora of deities and avatars, is now the largest of stable democracies, worldwide!

Unfortunately, Christianity has not succeeded in promoting democracy to any great extent in the governments of Islamic States, which largely remain autocratic theocracies. By the admission of Islamic thinkers, democracy is incompatible with Islam; but Pakistan, having accepted democracy to some extent, is still relatively unstable. Modernity awaits...

It seems to be conclusively clear that Mariological theology concerning Mary, Mother of Jesus, has been a moving stimulus in the promotion of women from relative obscurity in society to a major role in today's world, in politics, family understanding and cohesion, industry, legal matters, and in so many other aspects of modern life. <u>Mary is therefore the proof of the heretofore unsuspected necessity of having a viable feminine element in religion,</u> and by extension, a place in the everyday life of modern societies, several of which are still opening themselves to these possibilities.

Seeing the advantages gained by the application of Mariology, however, we may ask ourselves – what would be the situation if there were only to exist the male element in religion, and in society? What would be the results?

<u>Several results seem to present themselves:</u>

- **Legal systems** would be more prone to radical punishment for infractions, balanced judgements would lack. Thus, there would be stoning for adultery, ablation of hands for theft, flogging for drinking of alcohol, etc., as in Islam.

- **Pardons** as possibilities for infractions would be less, imprisonments would be more severe, resulting in family break ups, lack of wherewithal for survival would ensue, etc.

- **International dialogue** and understanding would be severely compromised, i.e. no United Nations, international agreements would be only in favour of the powerful; the weak or disadvantaged would suffer.

- **Support** for distressed individuals and countries would be non-existent. The crushing of these would be commonplace.

- **International relationships** would suffer. In the 20th century there were 52 wars, in most of which were involved non-democratic nations, though the greatest were fought by democracies against Nazism and Communism.

- **Family life** would be to the advantage of the husband only, who would rule by order and force, not by dialogue and understanding. This would cause lack of love among spouses and children, causing delinquency, drug addictions, family separations, etc. Such families would suffer immensely in non-democratic societies also, seeing that tenderness, understanding, dialogue, charity, hope and love – all feminine virtues – would not form part of the society in which they live. However, it is clear that much remains to be done in these matters in democratic societies, even today.

There still remains a lot to bring to perfection the unique effect of Mariology in modern society, and to this end many are working around the world. It is to be hoped that one day there may be a clear vision of the role of both men and women in the societies of the world, not forgetting that of the Catholic Church itself, which had defined, after many years of theological thought and prayer, the role of the Virgin Mary, Mother of Jesus, and Mother of the Church.

Although the Reformation had rejected the cult of Mary with the dogmas defined in her honour, yet it seems today that certain Protestant groups are opening themselves to a re-think of this problem. For instance, the Archbishop of Canterbury caused a lot of controversy in the UK by declaring, after a recent visit to Lourdes, that he is of the opinion that the Virgin had really appeared there.

Several churches in the States of the southern U.S. have now included images of Our Lady of Guadalupe there, due to the influx of Latin-Americans from southern countries, and in the UK, the ancient shrine of Our Lady of Walsingham, destroyed by Henry Vlll, has now been reopened, for Catholic and Anglican services.

Islam also honours Mary, Mother of Issa (Jesus), in its Qur'an, naming her 32 times. So maybe, just maybe, Our Lady may one day be a sort of bridge between Christianity and Islam. But who knows? And who can tell?

Is there anything about Our Lady in the present opinions of her own people, the Jews? No official information is as yet forthcoming, unfortunately, although individual Jewish folk who have accepted Jesus the Messiah have also begun to consider the role of his Mother in their lives.

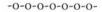

(To the serpent spoke Yahweh):
I will make you enemies of each other, you and the woman;
Your offspring and her offspring. It will crush
your head, and you will strike its heel.
(**Gen.3:15**)

The Lord himself will give you a sign:
"The ***maiden*** is with child,
And will soon give birth to a son, whom she will call Immanuel"
(**Is.7:24**)

When the appointed time came, God
sent his Son, born of a ***woman***,
Born a subject of the Law, to redeem the subjects of the Law,
And to enable us to be adopted as sons.
(**Gal.4:4-5**)

The mother of Jesus said "They have no wine".
Jesus said "***Woman***, ***why turn to me?***
My hour has not yet come"
(**Jn.2:4 -5**)

To his mother [Jesus] said "***Woman***, ***this is your son***".
To the disciple he said ***"This is your mother"***
(**Jn.19:26-27**)

A great sign appeared in heaven; A
woman, adorned with the sun,
Standing on the moon, and with the twelve stars on her head,
For a crown.
(**Rev.12:1**)

-o-o-o-o-o-o-o-

CHAPTER **18**

Jesus' Presence

Jesus Among His People

"I will be with you always... even to the end of this age"

These are the very last words spoken by Our Lord to his Apostles, immediately before his being taken up into heaven (**Lk.24:51; Mt.28:18-20**). They were preceded by a declaration of his own divinity *"All power in heaven and on earth has been given to me"* (**v. 18**), and *"Go therefore, make disciples of all the nations, baptising them in the name of the Father, and of the Son, and of the Holy Spirit,* (**v.19***), teaching them to observe all that I have commanded you"* (**v.20**). *And know, I will be with you always.......* etc".

It is of little importance whether these words were actually spoken by Our Lord to his Apostles in that form, or whether they had compiled a series of his words to present them as such. What matters is that they were absolutely convinced of his divinity, of the importance of the message he had come to bring, and that they had been commissioned to continue his marvellous work throughout the world. This is the Missionary Mandate as understood by all who refer to themselves as Christians, and is the reason why the larger and smaller denominations all have missions in countries which need the message of Jesus. But it is the last verse which has caused a lot of controversy among Christian groups – just **how** is Jesus to be with us, to the end of the age?

Although all denominations would agree that Jesus is with us in prayer, whether in groups or individually, by his Spirit, by his truth, by his inspirations etc etc, yet the Catholic Church, by the delegation of his authority in **Mt.16:13-20**, including the "power of the keys to bind and loose" (**v.19**), has decided through twenty centuries of theological thought and prayer, that Jesus is, in a very particular way with the Church he founded, present in the Sacramental System. However, since the upheaval of the 16th century Reformation, Protestant groups have distanced themselves from the whole System, most retaining only Baptism and the "Lord's Supper", the others having been eliminated as superstitions. Nevertheless……

The Catholic Church teaches that here are Seven Sacraments, decided by long and meaningful theological research. Each corresponds to an important aspect of human life, from birth to death, named in accordance with each aspect. In each Sacrament, the Church teaches that Jesus is there, present through the agency and actions of the priests of his Church, sanctifying the necessary outward actions, and giving the grace necessary to the person receiving the Sacrament to fulfil it completely. Thus, we take each in turn:

1) **BAPTISM** (**Jn.3:5-6**); Effects - removal of Original or Actual Sin; visible integration into the Mystical Body of Christ, the visible Church. Any person – even a non-Christian – can confer this Sacrament, provided that

the person conferring it wishes to do what the Church intends, and uses the correct Trinitarian formula.

2) **CONFIRMATION** (**Acts 2:1-12**); Effects – gift of the Spirit, a call to witness to the truth received at Baptism. Can be conferred only by a Bishop or by a delegated priest.

3) **PARDON** (**Jn.20:23**; **James 5:16**). Effects - reconciliation with the Lord, following his instructions, not just the human need and will to be pardoned by expressing such to God. Conferred by Bishop or priest.

4) **MATRIMONY** (**Mt.19:3-9**) Effects - a true imitation of the union of Christ and his Church (**Eph.5:25-27**); thus - no divorce is possible when there is a valid marriage (**Mt.19:1-6**). Conferred by Bishop, priest or deacon.

5) **LAST RITES** (or for the **SICK**) (**James 5:14-15**). Effects - preparation for death, or for strengthening in illness. Conferred by Bishops or priests.

6) **HOLY ORDERS** (**Lk.22:19-20**). Effects - perpetual continuation of the work of Our Lord, the priesthood *"Do this in memory of me"*. (See Chap.4 – The Covenants). For celibacy –see **Mt.19:10-12.** Conferred only by a Bishop.

7) **EUCHARIST** (**Mt.26:26-28**; **Lk.22:19-20**). Effects – The Real Presence of Jesus in every Mass- *"Take and eat, take and drink, this is my Body, this is my Blood"*. This is the logical conclusion of the dual natures of Christ, who speaks as the Second Person of the Trinity, not only as a man (Council of Chalcedon 451 AD). Celebrated only by Bishops and priests.

Throughout her long life, the Catholic Church, notwithstanding her many sins, has been very careful to imitate Our Lord in his relationships with the sheep of his flock. This is particularly so in her teaching of the Sacramental System, where every aspect of a person's life is considered to be sanctified by the presence of Christ. Each aspect is shown by the Sacraments, from birth to natural death. The following aspects of the Sacraments are intended to show this close cohesion between Jesus and his flock.

While Jesus was among the people in his country, run by the Roman Empire but led by the Jewish hierarchy, the Sanhedrin, the priestly class, the Pharisees and the Sadducees, he never made exception among those whom he had the chance to meet.

He was very fond of children, in fact he had to reproach his Apostles who had tried to drive them away. *"Let the little children come to me"*, he said, *"for it is for such as these that the kingdom of heaven was made"* (**Mt.18:1-7**; **Mk.10:13-16;** **Lk.18:15-17**), warning them against scandalising children, not causing them to be lost. Following Jesus' concerns for children, the early Church, according to Apostolic tradition, decided to baptise children as well as adults, according to Saints Ambrose and Augustine, among others. The baptism given to the "households" in **Acts 16:15, 33-34** also seems to refer to this early custom, although children are not expressly mentioned there. Today, Baptism is given to small children, even babies, to remove Original Sin, to include them in the visible Church founded by Jesus. Their parents accept the responsibilities to teach and bring them up in the Faith of their Baptism. It is a parental commitment.

Strengthening the Faith (Con-firm = Confirmation) is taken from **Acts 1:8**, where Jesus said to his Apostles just before his Ascension into heaven *"You will be my witnesses……to the ends of the earth"*. Witness to Jesus is thus one of the main characteristics of his Church. This has always been understood to be a Sacrament, where Jesus is spiritually present, giving the grace and force to carry on his work. Untold thousands of men and women, children, teachers, theologians, nuns, priests, missionaries, martyrs, and very humble folk from many countries, have been witnesses to Jesus during twenty centuries, many of whom are canonised Saints, already enjoying the bliss of the Kingdom in the presence of Almighty God.

Due to humanity's tendency to sin, it was inevitable that Jesus should encounter sinners. He forgave their sins, an action attributable to God alone (**Mt.9:1-8**; **Lk.5:17-26; Jn.8:3-11**). Before his trial, condemnation and death, Jesus had given his Apostles "authority over unclean spirits with power to cast them out, and to cure all kinds of diseases and sickness" (**Mt.10:1**). Now, after his death and resurrection, Jesus intends that this privilege of forgiving sins should continue in his Church through the work of the Apostles. He delegates to them this authority at his apparition on the day of his resurrection (**Jn. 20:19-23**). This Sacrament of Reconciliation (Pardon) is guaranteed by the gift of the Holy Spirit, and thus Jesus showed the manner by which it should be administered, accompanied by a certain satisfaction to be performed by the penitent, e.g. by prayer, works of charity, change of life, *("Go, and sin no more")*. This Sacrament is a continuation of the work of Jesus, and is a form of witness to his sure presence among us.

On creating "male and female", Almighty God intended that they should "become one body", to "be fruitful and multiply, fill the earth" (**Gen.1:26-28; 2:18-25**). Matrimony was always a blessing for the Jewish people, and the Church, sprung from Judaism, also considers it to be most holy. Unless there have been serious impediments to a valid marriage, there can be no divorce. Marriage is indeed a Sacrament, both because Jesus had declared it to be holy (**Mt.19:3-9**; **Mk.10:1-12**), and because it is a mystery, an imitation of the mystery of the mystical union of Christ and his Church (**Eph.5:25-33**), the Mystical Body of Christ. The encyclical ***Mystici Corporis Christi*** of Pope Pius Xll, in 1943 defines this.

(See Chap.1 – The Divine Plan).

So as to proclaim the arrival of the Kingdom after his having left the world, Jesus decided to leave others in his place. At the Passover with his Apostles in the Cenacle, after instituting the Holy Eucharist, Jesus gave them a serious command, to do as he had done, saying ***"Do this in memory of me"*** (**Lk.22:19**; **1Cor.11:17-26**). He speaks here as the Second Person of the Blessed Trinity, and his words must be taken seriously. In his "Memory" would mean unceasing continuity in the future. The Church has always considered this to be the Sacrament of Holy Orders, and those who receive it by ordination become priests, whose priesthood had been inaugurated by Jesus himself at the Passover meal. The priests of the Catholic Church have taken the place of those of the Old Testament, whose duty was to offer sacrifices of blood to Yahweh. The Jewish priesthood came to an end with the destruction of the Second Temple in 70 AD. In the New Testament, the priests offer the unbloody sacrifice of the Body and Blood of Jesus at every Mass, a mystery in itself. (See Chap.4 – The Covenants)

Through the Sacrament of the Sick the Church ministers to the sick or dying, as Jesus did. She is the world's most engaged single non-governmental organisation to this end with her hospitals, clinics, orphanages, schools for "special needs", or retirement homes, many of which bear the names of saints. This Sacrament's origin is based on Jesus' ministry, a care which obviously had been taken to heart by the early Church (**Jas.5:14-15**). It combines the two Sacraments of Pardon and Eucharist (called Viaticum = food for the journey home). In helping people to be reconciled with

God, to regain health, or to comfort the dying, this Sacrament operates miraculously in many cases; but always it is Jesus who is there among his people, caring for them through the care of his Church.

While each of the seven Sacraments bears the spiritual presence of Our Lord through the ministry of his Church, yet that of the Eucharist goes much further. The Church officially teaches that in the Eucharistic celebration Jesus is himself physically present, in a *sacramental* way. (See Chap.8 -Transubstantiation, and Chap. 9 – So, what is the Mass? for fullest information).

Sacramental means that the *substances* (the *essential natures of being* of the bread and wine) have been changed by the power of their Creator (in this case Jesus, the Second Person of the Trinity) into the *essential natures* of his own Body and Blood. In metaphysics, this is properly called *Transubstantiation*, the transformation of one *essential nature into another* by the creative power of God.

The *physical attributes* of bread (weight, colour, taste, composition), and those of wine (colour, composition, taste, weight) remain, it is their *essential nature,* their *inner reality* in each case, which has been changed.

On receiving Holy Communion at Mass, the person experiences the weight, taste, and composition of both bread and/or wine, but their *essential natures* have been changed into the *essential natures* of the Body and Blood of Our Lord. It is only by humble acceptance of this *mysterium fidei* (the mystery of faith) that the recipient can hope to understand the Eucharist.

For the Church, and for the spiritual life of all the faithful, the Eucharist is the Real Presence of Jesus among his people.

Notwithstanding the incoherencies of Protestantism concerning the Mass and the Eucharist, the first being mere superstition, the second being merely symbolic, the Catholic Church cannot, and will not, ever, diverge from her belief in Jesus' words, and her teaching, that this is his Body, that this is his Blood. As the Preface lll of the Sundays in Ordinary Time puts it *"you... fashioned for us a remedy out of mortality itself, that the cause of our downfall might become the means of our salvation"*. Our human mortality, fallen through Adam, has in fact been redeemed by the resurrected Jesus, the new Adam (**1Cor.15:22-23**).

When therefore Jesus had said, at the Last Supper – the First Mass – the words *"Take and eat, this is my Body"*, and *"Take and drink, this is my Blood"* (**Mt.26:26-28**; **Lk.22:19-20**), he in fact was inaugurating a new Covenant with human beings, giving a promise also which would be the continuation of his presence with humanity till the "end of the age" (**Mt.28:20**). This new Covenant is the Sacrament of the Eucharist. From the start of the Church, from the very earliest years, the Church has believed and taught this. (See Chap.4 – The Covenants)

As Vatican ll has said (*Lumen Gentium*, No.11) *"The Eucharist is the Source and Summit of the life of the Church"*, and it is by the Eucharist that the Church, and all the Sacraments, find their justification and completion. It was during the Last Supper that a New Covenant was inaugurated as part of two Sacraments.

This new concept and tradition commenced by Our Lord himself is the fulfilment of the ancient ones of the Old Testament. The former ones concerned the Jewish people exclusively, this New Covenant was divinely instituted so as to reach all nations and peoples in the world.

The belief of the Catholic Church in the Sacramental System is firmly rooted in its Traditions, which preceded the compilation of the Bible, in Biblical teaching itself, and in her Councils through the centuries. She believes that when arrives "the end of the age" (**Mt.28:20**), and there takes place the Judgement promised by Jesus (**Mt.25:31-46**), there will be both Retribution and Reward. Retribution means punishment and separation from God, but in Reward, the elect "will be as He is, for we will see him as he is" (**1 Jn.3:2**), i.e. they will share in His divine nature in the fullest sense, called in theology the Beatific Vision. Not "vision" in secular terms, but rather "Inclusion" in the Nature of Almighty God himself.

No human being can see God Himself, obstructed as we are by our mere humanity. Jesus knew this, but has fashioned the way to do so in a way that only God Himself could have imagined. He has left us the Holy Eucharist, which we can certainly understand as being God Himself in *sacramental* form (**Mt.26:26-28**; **Lk.22:19-20**). Because of this possibility, there are Adoration Chapels, Corpus Christi celebrations, and Benediction of the Blessed Sacrament, in which we can contemplate God in sacramental form, and in the Reserve of the Tabernacle there is always the possibility of "Visits" to the Blessed Sacrament at any time when the church is open. It is up to us to continue to offer thanks to Our Lord for His generosity, and to deepen our acceptance of the reality of His Presence in the Eucharist, particularly when we prepare to receive Him.

-o-o-o-o-o-o-o-

> A mighty God is the Lord,
> A great king above all gods.
> In his hand are the depths of the earth;
> The heights of the mountains are his.

To him belongs the sea, for he made it,
And the dry land, shaped by his hands.

Come in; let us bow and bend low;
Let us kneel before the God who made us,
For he is our God and we
The people who belong to his pasture,
The flock that is led by his hand.

(Ps. 95(94), vs.3-7)

-o-o-o-o-o-o-o-o-

CHAPTER 19
Jesus Lifted Up

"*When I am lifted up………..*"

….. *I shall draw all men to myself*" (**Jn.12:32**)

Jesus had uttered the prophetic words above, after his entry into Jerusalem on a young donkey (**Mk.11:1-7**), when the crowd had acclaimed him (**Mk.11:9-10**). He had then gone to nearby Bethany to pass the night (**Mk.11:11**), and had returned to Jerusalem the next day, where he had celebrated the Passover meal (**Lk.22:14-20; Mk.14:12-31**), with his Apostles.

He had then been arrested in the garden of Gethsemane (**Jn.18:1-11; Mk.14:32-52**), and been condemned to death by Pilate (**Mk.15:15; Jn.19:12-16**). At his crucifixion (**Jn.19:17-22; Lk.23:33-46**), Jesus was indeed lifted up from the earth.

But what indeed did his words mean?

In the Old Testament, the book of **Numbers 21:6-9** gives a fairly good explanation of this being *"lifted up"*:

In one episode during their forty-year journeying through the harsh desert of Arabia, many Jews had died from snakebite. Upon the recommendation of Yahweh, Moses had made a bronze serpent and put it on a pole. Anyone bitten had only to look at the bronze serpent to be cured and live.

This event clearly is analogy of Jesus on the Cross. As he himself had said some time before: ***"Whoever sees the Son and believes in him has eternal life, and I will raise him on the last day"*** (**Jn.6:40**). The word "see" would of course mean a proper discernment and recognition that this crucified man is really the Son of God, sent by the Father.

An example of this is in **Jn.12:21b**, when some non-Jewish Greeks, who had also come to celebrate the Passover (as many non-Jewish sympathisers did at that time, though remaining non-Jewish thru rejection of circumcision), asked to see Jesus. Perhaps they would have been the first to "see" Jesus, apart from the Roman soldiers present at the crucifixion, e.g. the centurion and his troop (**Mk. 15:39; Lk.23:47**) who had exclaimed *"Really, this man was a Son of God!"* (though omitting the theological interpretation).

Through the following centuries, let us imagine Jesus on the Cross. He sees the world's peoples coming and looking at him. Many accept his claims, his reality, his teaching - but many reject him. Many come just to observe him on the Cross, fascinated by this Person. He looks at each group, at each nation, each religious leaning, and speaks to them:

"Welcome, you who have believed in me from the very start, you who are still my Church, the One Church I founded with Simon as its head (**Mt.16:15-19**). *I had changed his name from Simon to Rock – "Peter" – to be the firm foundation I built on, for all time, unchangeable but growing as peoples and their understandings and mentalities evolve. You have kept the Faith intact. Notwithstanding your many human weaknesses, Hades has not prevailed. The Saints of all nations and peoples are among you, you will receive the fullness of my Kingdom".*

Welcome also, you who believe in me, but not in the fullness of the Faith taught by my Apostles, but rather rely on the traditions of those you follow. How can there be one "Lord, one Faith, one Baptism, one God and Father of all" (**Eph.4:5-6**), *when there are presently *47,000 different interpretations of it today? Dearly beloved, while there is still time, I beseech you, inform yourselves, forgive past injustices, return to the one Church I have prepared for you, realise that scattering cannot promote unity* (**Mt.12:30b**). *I suffer for you, my beloved, and I am awaiting your return, anxiously.* [*2018 findings of Gordon-Conwell Evangelical Seminary in U.S.A.]

O followers of Islam, I hopefully await your coming to my light. Your founder had attempted, but had only badly and partially understood my reality and my message, the road to redemption which I had come to announce. There is indeed only one God, one who is compassionate Love, who offers sincere fraternity. You call me Issa, and I am indeed Son of the Most High, born of His will, not of human agency, as your own Book teaches. You too must seek more deeply into my message, there is no other way for you to enter my kingdom. My love goes out to you, and I am yet awaiting yours. And remember my words: "He who lives by the sword shall die by the sword" (Mt.26:52).

Dearly beloved brothers and sisters, you who believe in Brahman the Most High, you have mightily tried, yet are still searching. Indeed, the One True God has come among you. Look upon Him on this Cross, ultimate proof of God who is Love himself, who has gone to such lengths to prove it. My Spirit still circulates among you, listen to him, follow his inspirations. You will realise at last that you are loved beyond measure, and are called to share life eternal in my kingdom.

Can I not love you, O peoples who are Buddhist, Confucianist, Shintoist, as well as the many offspring from your beliefs? Of course, I do! I ask you to look up and see the reality of the absolute Love of the living God, which goes beyond mere belief. Death is but mere passage to eternity. Man lives just once, and if life has been rightly lived, man can enter into the endless joy I have promised. Open your hearts, come to me! I have been waiting for you for centuries now, and to the end of this age I will always be here waiting for you!

My dear indigenous peoples of Africa, the Americas, India, Australia, and others, my love extends to you in a very special way. I know that you have faith in the High God of your cultures, and here before you is the proof that your faith invites you to go further, to see here the God-come-among-you. Be blessed in your growing faith, let it come to full flower in me and my message. My life has been for you, and I await your love in the fullest measure possible. May you be blessed in your efforts to find me.

To you, my friends who profess not to believe in your Creator and Redeemer, let me say however that the Father-Creator himself believes in you. He believes and knows that you carry the germ of immortality in you, that the doubts you nurture are quite normal, that in every day and in every way, there are revealing hints of His presence. The intervention of pure chance is inadequate to explain the world's order and its complexity, nor does an impersonal Intelligence suffice to explain anything. The Author of all is indeed Divine Love, whose Word has been sent to reveal Him. Observe, consider its reality upon this Cross. You are yet unfree, but to find the real freedom you desire, come, observe the Son who believes in you, that you too may believe in Him.

My dearest brothers and sisters of the line of Abraham, I cry to you from my heart, open yours and come to your Brother on the Cross! I have fulfilled all the prophecies of our people, I have accomplished the Law of Moses to the full, (Mt.5:18) *and have not refused the sufferings and death of which great Isaiah spoke. I live for ever now before our God, whose very Being I fully share. Await no more for the arrival of the Messiah, I have already come, and will come again, in glory next time, with all the angels of God. Seek no more, I am before you, and I await joyfully for the day when you will accept the one Truth which can save you and all humanity. You are so dear to me, and I wish you to share the happiness of my Father's Kingdom! Come, I call and await you!*

… and with these words, he bowed his head, and breathed his last. (**Lk.23:46**).

"Into your hands, Lord, I commend my spirit!"

-o-o-o-o-o-o-o-

Were you there when they crucified my Lord?
Were you there when they crucified my Lord?
Oh, sometimes it causes me to tremble, tremble, tremble.
Were you there when they crucified my Lord?

Were you there when they nailed him to the tree?
Were you there when they nailed him to the tree?
Oh, sometimes it causes me to tremble, tremble, tremble.
Were you there when they nailed him to the tree?

Were you there when they laid him in the tomb?
Were you there when they laid him in the tomb?
Oh, sometimes it causes me to tremble, tremble, tremble.
Were you there when they laid him in the tomb?

(Good Friday spiritual hymn)

-o-o-o-o-o-o-o-

CHAPTER **20**

The Catholic Family

Whatever Happened to the Catholic family?

Our present confusing, confused, and crazy world has been built upon the past, and though it is not correct, nor right, to assign blame ("Judge not..." – **Mt.7:1-7**), yet it is necessary to know the past so as to understand the present, and to prepare the future. As the Spanish-American philosopher Santayana once said *"Those who do not know the past are condemned to repeat it"*. So, on to the past, but first let's note the most important modernist and atheistic philosophers of the 19th century – Nietzsche, Kant, Heidegger, Hegel, Marx, whose thought and writings have most influenced our world of today. At the same time, I admit that this theme deserves a book, or a library, to get to the bottom of the question. It's just an effort!

Now, as to understand just who we are, on to 1900!

1900 – All the ruling heads of Europe are blood-related to the ageing Queen Victoria of England, whose "age" is rapidly ending. Marxism is waiting offstage for its turn, a result of anger against the cruelties of the European Industrial Revolution. Militaristic Prussian Germany is rattling its sabres, the aeroplane of 1902 will graduate from the accustomed "oohs" and "ahhs", to become a chosen instrument of war, from the air.

The Catholic Church is still then under the leadership of Leo XIII, who in 1893 had forbidden the Vulgate [Latin] Bible to be translated into modern languages. But the Catholic family doesn't mind, thinking, most probably, *"The Bible is for Protestant Bible-thumpers. We have the true Church to tell us right from wrong. We have the [obligatory] Sunday Mass in Latin, the Rosary, the Angelus, the morning and night prayers, Grace before and after meals. Nothing to worry about, really. We're in God's hands!"* This indicates the serious and widespread divisions among Christians in the 1900s.

But Catholic parents are happy, the children obey, go to Mass with them; religious vocations are not really a problem, Church and family are respected and in good standing in the community. But, <u>there's no Bible in the Catholic families!</u>

<u>1914-1918</u> – WW1. The 'war to end all wars' breaks over Europe and over the world. Pius X dies (of a broken heart?). Germany loses, Lenin and collaborators install Marxist Communism in Russia, the Royal family there is massacred, the Muslim Ottoman Empire ends shortly afterwards. European civilisation begins to unravel, the League of Nations is set up.

The moral authority of the Church begins to diminish, her advice to the leaders of nations is ignored, millions of Christians of all denominations are killed. Europe begins to forget its past as nations built by the Church. The Catholic family continues on its traditional way, living its particular conventions. Still, <u>no Bible is in Catholic families</u> - that's for Protestants! <u>*"We have our Faith to guide us!"*</u> is the unwritten code of the family. Children and youth still obey, no problem is there. The Church slumbers, and life goes on as usual. The League of Nations proves to be largely ineffectual. But......

Germany re-arms under Hitler, the League of Nations is ineffective to stop this. Europe is taken by surprise.

1936-1939 – The Spanish Civil War breaks out, Fascists aided by Germany against Republican Communists. Fascists win, this war being just a prelude to WW ll.

1939-1945 – **World War ll.** Germany takes over many European countries, makes a pact of friendship with Japan, which invades far-Eastern countries. The US enters the war after the attack on Pearl Harbour in 1941. Millions are killed world-wide, including 6 million Jews in Nazi death-camps. D-day in 1945 causes the War in Europe to end, and soon after 2 atom-bombs on Japan's two cities end the war in the East. The League of Nations being disbanded, the UN is set up in New York.

The Catholic Church had become aware of the poverty of Catholic family prayer and the education of children in the Faith, and so Pius Xll permitted the Vulgate to be translated into modern languages in 1943, by ***Divino Afflante Spiritu***, (*By the Spirit's Inspiration*). Basically, the family had not changed nor progressed. Parents had begun to lose faith in society, through the unending wars and upheavals. Women had begun to take men's places in industry and manufacture due to the war effort (Rosie the Riveter!). Society began to be shaken, Church marriages and religious vocations began to diminish, divorces became more common. But the family continued in its traditional way – [obligatory] Latin Mass on Sunday, the Rosary (less often), morning and night prayers, Grace before and after meals. – This was around 1950.

1945-1991 – The Cold War between Russia and the West set in. NATO as a deterrent to Russian aggression was set up.

1950-1953 – the Korean War, (technically, this is not over as yet), of Communist inspiration, followed by…..

1956-1975 - the Vietnamese War, also of Communist inspiration, won by Ho Chi Minh, lost by the US.

This continuous series of wars – 52 in all in the 20th century! – severely shook the Catholic Church. Many of its children had been lost, vocations plummeted. But the Catholic family continued as usual, traditional and conventional - *bless them*! No serious new proposals on lay spirituality came out, even through the Council Vatican ll (1962-65). The first modern English Bible was published in 1966, but few guides were offered as to its reading or use. Many families bought a copy, but were unaccustomed to using it, and mostly kept it on a shelf, to show that they had one. Sadly, the Bible continued to be a stranger to lay Catholic thought, which still seems to be the general situation to this day of 2020, even though many efforts have been made to correct this. Most families remain unaware that it was the Catholic Church which had filtered and compiled all proposed competing books since 367AD, for the New Testament, and 400AD for the Old Testament. These were ratified by the Council of Trent, (1546-1563). (See Chap.13 – Sola Scriptura).

Years of the 1950s – Escaping from the restrictions of WW2, these years saw new thinking among boisterous young people world-wide, including Catholic youth. Rock bands, and the 'new music' spread and grew like mushrooms – Bill Haley's "Comets", L'il Richard, Elvis Presley, the Rolling Stones, the Beatles, Big Bopper, Abba – to name just a few among the hundreds which came out. Parents, accustomed to the 'Swing Bands' of the

40's – Artie Shaw, Glen Miller, Benny Goodman, the Dorseys – couldn't understand this music, couldn't control it, and finally gave up trying. Then came…..

1965-1977 – Sexual Revolution – Woodstock – the Pill(s) and other means of artificial contraception, began to be known.

7/1968 – Seeing the widespread threat of uncontrolled sexuality, and advised by a panel of experts, Paul Vl issued ***Humanae Vitae***, condemning artificial contraception. This was not accepted by many priests and Bishops around the world, and two months later those in Canada in **9/1968** issued their *Winnipeg Statement* against the Pope's encyclical.

The Sexual Revolution percolated into all countries and all cultures. The use of condoms, sterilets, and the Pill(s) made sex into a largely recreational activity, which had begun years before ***Humanae Vitae***. The encyclical influenced Catholic youth negatively, turning them against the teachings of the Church. The clergy were influenced by this, and Catholic families continued on their traditional and conventional ways of living their faith, while the Ark of Peter was being swamped.

1962-1965 – The Council Vatican 2 permitted Holy Mass in local languages. Latin was given a secondary importance, but the Sunday obligation remained, and the usual prayers and Rosary continued in Catholic families. Vocations continued to fall disastrously, recreational sex became the norm, strip-clubs bloomed, shacking-up, divorce, concubinage became far more common, Hollywood-style. In the meantime, the Catholic families continued as they had always been taught, bravely trying to stem the tide and protect their children against confusing and impossible odds.

2020 et seq – There have been added to their confusion and despair the various gay, transgender and hybrid movements. Porn is on every child's computer, abortion and euthanasia – even of the very young – is rampant, and may soon be on demand. But the family continues to pray the usual prayers, use the Rosary, and go to Mass, all the while lamenting the absence of the young. It is rare that a personal relationship with Jesus is ever encouraged among the children of the family.

What's the situation of today's family?

Many, many families have declared their disappointment concerning their young people. *"They don't pray any more, don't go to Mass; they hang out for ungodly hours. Some are on drugs, some have shacked-up, some have babies which are unbaptised, some are gay...... What on earth is going on?"* They say *"We seem to have lost an entire generation! It's as if my life has been a waste of time!"*. So, let us try to organise our thoughts!

We start with the children:

A child, from infancy to about 12-13, is nevertheless a "captive" in its home, always obliged to obey Mom and Dad, with the risk of some sort of punishment for disobedience. The child may be sweet, mostly obedient, somewhat egoistic, but always harbours a sort of childish resentment on being obliged to follow orders from parents. This resentment will sometimes reveal itself by disobedience, which is really a childish way of asserting its own independence. Some parents consult child psychologists to understand, but most parents don't, nor do they ask opinions of their children, *"He's too young to think for himself!"* they'd say, and as the saying went *"Children should be seen, and not heard!"*.

Upon reaching 12-13, or even sooner, **puberty** kicks in, with greater need for independence. Then the "trouble" starts, as Mom and Dad just cannot understand why Jimmy (or Jenny) is so disobedient and self-seeking. *"Didn't we feed them, clothe them, protect them, send them to good schools, teach them the morning and night prayers, Grace before and after meals? Weren't they altar-boys and altar-girls? Didn't we pray the Rosary together every day? Really, we can't understand our boy/girl. He/she is so **different** now! Quite unlike what we expected them to be!"* Indeed, parents have a hard time!

It must be understood that today's youth are not like they were in the 40's and 50's. They are products of many modernist philosophies, one of which is the Sexual Revolution of the 60's and 70's. They are also heavily influenced by the media, by their peers at school and particularly in Universities, which often teach ***"It is forbidden to forbid".*** In other words, today's youth are by no means of a traditional bent, they are totally new and out of touch with traditional Catholicism. The years of the 50's or 60's were the ages of the Flower-Power movements, the Hippies and free love, the love-ins, the great youth demonstrations of Woodstock etc etc. The war in Vietnam also had its influence [*think Jane Fonda*] and most in the West had lost faith in their governments and in themselves. Parents continued bravely on, but not understanding.....

Catholics, and Catholicism in general, have been living <u>in a mould of convention and obligation for the last century</u>, and particularly in the last 70 years. Being Catholic has meant being obliged to attend Sunday Mass (upon pain of mortal sin if missed), paying Church dues, and saying the usual prayers. All well and good, but these were the basics. We prayed the Rosary and the normal prayers, but 70 years ago few families had and used Bibles, although the first modern English Bible had come out a few years after World War Two.

Practising Catholics saw Bibles as the job of the specialists, and in fact the Church did not encourage reading or praying with the Bible, seeing what that had done to fragment the Church into the many dissident denominations, which had taught their "free interpretation of the Bible". (According to the 2018 findings of the Gordon-Conwell Evangelical Seminary in the US, there are now approximately 47,000 non-Catholic denominations in the world, some being only Christian by name).

Combining the Church's inertia of the last century concerning lay spirituality, the traditional and conventional Catholic family method of living its Faith, the new thinking among young people concerning their identity, their hunger to become freer and more independent, it is not surprising that young folk in droves have fallen away from family customs and even from the Church. When the child reaches 14, all the prayers and Church manners taught by his parents are interpreted only as means of obedience and obligation, old-fashioned, and he throws them out, in the name of independence.

The Rosary itself is seen as boring, it becomes just like the interminable clicking of a bicycle's chain, going around and round, meaning nothing. And the same goes for Sunday-Mass, just nothing - boring, is the usual opinion. Besides, given the tendency of modern youth to demand instant answers and results (one of the strengths of the digital age!), they diverge completely from their parents, and follow their own road. They confess that they love their parents, but do not feel obliged to do as they say, nor follow as they did. Indeed, **Independence rocks!**

This means that many parents remain disappointed in their children, and as a result the Church has lost many families. Non-practising youth have become non-practicing adults, and the families which the young could have started never see the light of day. Concubinage has become a style of life, babies, if any, will neither be baptised, confirmed, nor married. Lost generations perhaps, and the loss to the Church of vocations is another of these sad results. What can be done?

It seems to be clear that the age-old traditions and obligations and conventions in Catholic families have had their day. They served well in the past, now maybe another method can be tried, perhaps by adaptation.

The usual night and morning prayers taught to small children should never be omitted, with <u>both parents participating</u>. Sunday's Mass should be an occasion of celebrating family togetherness and love for Our Lord, not just as an obligation under obedience. Above all, <u>a personal relationship with Our Lord and Our Lady should be seriously sought</u>. Many young people have only vague ideas about either, as their parents themselves hadn't learnt, and so couldn't teach them. It is not enough to teach the Rosary, one or two short decades can be followed by the associated readings and discussions.

<u>*Catholic families should go back to the roots of their faith, by use of the Bible in the family at regular appointed times. Family prayer of 15 minutes each time should include all in the family, three or four times a week. Bible passages should be brief, reflected and commented on, by each and all present, even the very young. Giving an opportunity to children to speak their minds would prepare them to defend their faith in later years, so as not to be mocked or preyed upon, in Secondary*</u>

School or University. All this should improve the quality and purpose of Catholic family life.

To understand how to go about this, the Jewish people gives us an example. For about 4000 years or so they have kept their identity, surviving kingdoms, empires, kings and emperors, ostracism and pogroms, wars and slaughterings, holocausts, loss of their original country from 70AD to 1948 AD. And yet they have kept their heads above the terrible things done to them through the ages.

Today they are again in possession of their original land, and have become not only the only democratic country in the Middle East, but also one of the world's top innovators of scientific endeavour. They have won over 150 Nobel Prizes, more than any other country, populations compared. What has been their strength, their secret? Can we learn from them?

Many Jews of today may have become agnostics or atheists, some may practice only rarely, but all revere their past and keep its traditions. They may have been waiting for the Messiah for centuries, but their secret lies in their faith, their unshakeable conviction that God had chosen them to be his people, notwithstanding all that history has thrown at them. One of the first books of the Bible says this:

> *Hear, O Israel, the Lord our God is one Lord; and you shall love the Lord our God with all your heart, and with all your soul, and with all your might. And these words which I command you today shall be upon your heart; and you shall teach them diligently to your children, and shall talk of them when you sit in your house, and when you walk by the way, and when you lie down, and when you rise.* (**Deut.6:4-7**)

Many other biblical texts reinforce their identity, and most non-Jews have heard about the Jewish feasts of Passover (from which comes the Christian Easter), Rosh Hashanah (Jewish New Year), Yom Kippur (Day of Atonement), and Hanukah (Feast of Lights, re-dedication of the Temple), as well as their observance of the Shabbat, the day of rest and prayer.

But how many Christians can explain the reality of just why we believe in Jesus, that he is in fact the long-awaited Messiah of the Jews, where he came from, what biblical texts refer to him, and what will happen next in our history, as he himself promised? We must admit that in this both parents and children are woefully ignorant, so here are some of the most important texts about Jesus, which would help both parents and children to develop a personal relationship with our Lord. <u>**Use of the family Bible is not only recommended, but is absolutely indispensable,**</u> texts to be read in turn by each child in the family. As St. Jerome said *"Ignorance of the Scriptures is ignorance of Christ"*. Here now is Jesus in the Bible:

> **Jesus would be born of a Virgin (<u>Is.7:14</u>)** – and He was (<u>Mt.1:18-25</u>; <u>Lk.1:34-38</u>).
>
> **He would be born in Bethlehem (Micah 5:2)** – and He was (<u>Lk.2:1-20</u>; <u>Mt.2:1-6</u>).
>
> **He would be taken into Egypt (<u>Hosea 11:1</u>)** – and He was (<u>Mt.2:15</u>).
>
> **He would heal the sick, making people whole (<u>Is.25:6-9, 61:1-3</u>)** – and He did (<u>Mt.8:1-34</u>; <u>Jn.9:1-41</u>).
>
> **He would be rejected (<u>Ps.118:22-23</u>)** – and He was (<u>Acts 4:10-12</u>)

He would suffer like no other (Is.53:1-12) – and He did suffer (Mt.27:1-54; Lk.23:13-49).

He would be crucified (Ps.22:1-18) – and He was (Mt.27:32-38; Mk.15:23-27).

He would die for our sins (Is.53:4-7) – and He did (Jn.11:50-51).

He would be raised from the dead (Ps.16:9-11; Is.53:10-12) – and He was (Mt.28:1-10; Mk.16:9-20).

He will come again (Mt.24:29-31; Mk.13:24-27) – This will arrive when God wishes it…..

The texts above are merely given as guides, there are many more – Parables, Beatitudes, etc - which parents can search for themselves and for the good of their family. It is to be hoped that parents would interest themselves more deeply in the sacred history of our Faith and be guided by it, getting away from the attitudes of conventionality and obligation which has been their way of living the Faith in past years. The Catholic Church can certainly learn from the Separated Brethren!

Just as the Jewish people have successfully done for so many centuries, today's Catholic families must accept their responsibilities about Faith, and share it with their children. They must be more careful about the interior lives of their children, to realise that *"giving them God"* must also be as important as giving them education, clothing, nourishment, and protection. It is to be feared that if such changes are not started and implemented, more future generations will be lost, just as those of the present seem to have been. Home-schooling, with its problems of adaptation, seems to be one of the bravest and best replies to the insistent tendency to paganise Catholic children in the ever-present secular society.

There have been serious results affecting the Church in general, and the Catholic family in particular, since the _Winnipeg Statement in Canada_ was published in September 1968, just two months after the promulgation of **Humanae Vitae.**

The Statement basically states that _**lay Catholics, having considered carefully the prohibition of artificial contraception as ruled by Humanae Vitae, were unable to follow the tenets of the Statement, and so were permitted to follow their own consciences, using the methods they choose in conscience, to regulate births in their families. Spiritual Directors would see to it that they were well informed, and that lay Catholics could choose in good conscience**_. The genie was clearly out of the bottle, notwithstanding the hopeful intentions of the Bishops that the laity would choose with good consciences.

Following are the most offending articles of the Statement.

17. It is a fact that a certain number of Catholics, although admittedly subject to the teaching of the encyclical, find it either extremely difficult or even impossible to make their own all elements of this doctrine. In particular, the argumentation and rational foundation of the encyclical, which are only briefly indicated, have failed in some cases to win the assent of men of science, or indeed of some men of culture and education who share in the contemporary empirical and scientific mode of thought. We must appreciate the difficulty experienced by contemporary man in understanding and appropriating some of the *points of this encyclical, and we must make every effort to learn from the insights of Catholic scientists and intellectuals, who are of undoubted loyalty to Christian truth, to the Church and to the authority of the Holy See. Since they are not denying any point of divine and Catholic faith nor rejecting the teaching authority of the Church, these Catholics should not be considered or consider themselves, shut off from the body of the faithful. But they should remember that their good faith will be dependent on a sincere self-examination to determine the true motives and grounds for such <u>suspension of assent</u> and on continued effort to understand and deepen their knowledge of the teaching of the Church.*

25. *In the situation we described earlier in this statement (par. 17) the confessor or counsellor must show sympathetic understanding and reverence for the sincere good faith of those who fall in their effort to accept some point of the encyclical.*

26. *Counsellors may meet others who, accepting the teaching of the Holy Father, find that because of particular circumstances they are involved in what seems to them a clear conflict of duties, e.g., the reconciling of conjugal love and responsible parenthood with the education of children already born or with the health of the mother. In accord with the accepted principles of moral theology, if these persons have tried sincerely but without success to pursue a line of conduct in keeping with the given directives, <u>they may be safely assured that, whoever honestly chooses that course which seems right to him, does so in good conscience.</u>*

34. *We conclude by asking all to pray fervently that the Holy Spirit will continue to guide his Church through all darkness and suffering. We, the People of God, cannot escape this hour of crisis, but there is no reason to believe that it will create division and despair. The unity of the Church does not consist in a bland conformity in all ideas, but rather in a union of faith and heart, in submission to God's will and* *a humble but honest and ongoing search for the truth. That unity of love and faith is founded in Christ, and as long as we are true to Him nothing can separate us. We stand in union with the Bishop of Rome the successor of Peter, the sign and contributing cause of our unity with Christ and with one another. But this very union postulates such a love of the Church that we can do no less than to place all of our love and all of our intelligence at its service. If this sometimes means that in our desire to make the Church more intelligible and more beautiful, we must, as pilgrims do, falter in the way or differ as to the way, no one should conclude that our common faith is lost or our loving purpose blunted. The great Cardinal Newman once wrote: "Lead kindly light amidst the encircling gloom". We believe that the Kindly Light will lead us to a greater understanding of the ways of God and the love of man.*

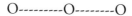

When this Statement was published, it was acclaimed by many, who considered it democratic and worthy of Canada. Lay associations praised it as an outstanding example of the respect that the Catholic Church had for families, for their difficult problems in a changing world, and for women in particular. So far so good, they claimed, and considered outrageous the mere idea that Pope Paul VI could insist on the Church's teaching on the immorality of artificial contraception!

From 1965-1977 the sexual revolution was dismembering the divorce laws across the world, popular culture had taken a decisive turn towards accepting pre-marital sexual activity as mere recreation, and **Humanae Vitae** had become "the most reviled document in the entire history of the papacy" (Fr.R.de Souza, in 2018). Even though the encyclical was defended by many Catholics who saw the dangers involved in its rejection, yet its non-acceptance is still current in Canada, in 2020, and the Statement remains un-retracted to this day. In fact, the vast majority of Catholics in Canada are even unaware of the Statement's existence, but the collective memory certainly allows its ambiguity to be put into practice.

Paul Vl, Pope and un-recognised prophet, was canonised in 2018. Indeed, *"The word of God is living and active. It cuts more finely than any two-edged sword"* (Heb.4:12).

It seems to be clear that a wrong turn was taken in publishing the Statement in 1968, although no doubt it was done in the hope that the Catholic laity would be wise enough to form their consciences with the aid of their Counsellors. In this those who published it were mistaken, having forgotten that most folk tend to auto-justify their actions and decisions, and the sad effects of the Statement on the Catholic family have been felt for some time. This worrisome situation could possibly be remedied should it be decided to publish an official retraction. Were this to be done, it would most probably bolster the opinion in a positive way which the general public, and Catholics in particular, have of their leaders.

Here now are some of the sad effects that the Winnipeg Statement, in rejecting outright *Humanae Vitae*, has had on the family life of Catholics. They had been unforeseen, but are now in the public gaze....

Some of the Unforeseen Results of the Rejection of *Humanae Vitae*

1) Many Catholic layfolk have decided that, since the Bishops have rejected *Humanae Vitae*, why should they accept it? Not having

a properly formed conscience, they have taken matters into their own hands, and they too have rejected it.

2) Many have simply left the Church, causing also a diminishing of children's numbers for catechism and Mass attendance.

3) Church funds and incomes have also drastically diminished.

4) Not having been properly formed in family prayer, non-practicing parents may not know how to pray with their children except, one hopes, for the conventional morning and night-time prayers, Graces at meals, and perhaps the Rosary.

5) Mass attendance has become largely sporadic for many, except for Christmas and Easter, and the occasional funeral.

6) Baptisms, Confirmations, Marriages have seriously diminished.

7) Diminishing of vocations, partly due to a lack of intelligent family prayer and distancing from the Church.

8) The young cannot defend their faith in school, risk being mocked, bullied, or ostracised, and bow to peer pressure.

9) Unrelenting paganisation of the young has led to drugs, porn, shacking-up, unbaptised babies, and lost generations.

10) De-Christianisation of the young is in progress, and will probably get worse.

11) The number of young people at Mass, even on Sundays, has been steadily diminishing, year after year.

12) The sexual revolution continues to take its toll, and not many youngsters go to Confession any more.

13) In this digital age, young folk, not having firm foundations in faith, will be prone to accept anyone and anything which may seem to give sense to their life. This will be one of the family priorities to be addressed.

14) The practice of liberal secularism has been given a great boost by the Winnipeg Statement.

15) The unhappiness of parents concerning their dashed hopes for their children is incalculable.

16) Single-parent "families" are becoming more commonplace, and are encouraged by rampant secularism.

17) There is a common and noticeable avoidance of Catholic priests by formerly-practising Catholic families.

18) Moral values having diminished, young people of both sexes distrust one another's motives in friendship; serious betrothals are rare, resulting in solid bases for marriage becoming a risky undertaking.

There are many other results, but it is up to the families themselves and the hierarchy to get their act together, to proclaim a most serious and meaningful change of heart, to get their priorities right. Unless begun with a deep understanding of its importance, it is quite possible that the Catholic family would risk losing more of its young people, and an advancement in spirituality, as Jesus would wish, would be merely a wishful pipe dream.

While the above may seem to be overly negative, yet it is clear that the hierarchy has been trying to get control of the situation, and has published several documents which they hope will give Catholic families the courage to listen to the voice of the Church, personified by their authority, that they may assent to this voice, and live their Catholic lives as God himself would wish. Here now are the documents issued, which can be found through the CCCB in Ottawa, showing that the Winnipeg Statement does not have the last word:

1969 Declaration on Family Life (this called for a deeper treatment of conscience; not the W. Statement).

1973 Statement on the Formation of Conscience

1993 Statement by the CCCB Executive Committee "An Integral Vision".

2008 Statement "Liberating Potential".

2018 Statement "The Joy of Married Love" (CCCB Doctrine Commission).

NB: An attempt under secret ballot by the Canadian Catholic Bishops to retract the Statement in 1998 did not pass, and up to 2020 it remains in force.

Humanae Vitae had mixed positive and negative results, as seen by the following instances:

The Netherlands: Humanae Vitae was mostly disregarded by the Dutch. The magisterium was not very strict, the medical profession mostly disregarded it. The only group that was very outspoken and against the Encyclical were the "Dolle Mina's" with their statement: *baas in eigen buik*. (Master of your own womb).

Bishops of the USA: Saw the Encyclical as an 'ideal' in their Statement. The laity had to choose in conscience.

Russia: Russian physicians were solidly against the Encyclical.

South America: The Bishops here mainly accepted the Encyclical; some cautioned acceptance, few rejected it.

Germany: The Bishops were ambiguous as to acceptance, layfolk accepted it.

Austria: Acceptance in general by the Bishops and layfolk.

France (2020): Originally the Bishops were divided in its acceptance; but the Encyclical is a dead letter now.

Australia: The Encyclical was authoritative, but lay Catholics could now choose artificial contraception in conscience.

As one commentator on **Humanae Vitae** put it "In 1968 the Catholic Church came of age". Pope Paul VI was so shaken by the mixed world receptions he received concerning Humanae Vitae, that in his remaining ten years of life he published no further encyclicals, limiting himself only to several Motu Propios. His successor Pope John-Paul I mysteriously died after being one month in office, and it was left to Pope St. John-Paul II to continue the fight of clarification concerning the Encyclical, trying to find the relationships between authoritative objective pronouncements and their subjective applications. In this he cannot be said to have completely succeeded. In **Veritatis Splendor** (1993) he rejects theological trends which disregard the absolute character of the Church's moral norms prohibiting intrinsically evil acts, and he repudiates ethical theories that make morality subjective.

[A short reflection on the role of conscience] – the concept of ***synderesis*** – the formation of the moral conscience.

St Thomas Aquinas played a significant role in clarifying the concept of conscience and the theoretical problems connected with it. He assigned to ***synderesis*** principally a cognitive role, arguing that [all] human beings have a fundamental grasp of right and wrong, which is infallible.

St Thomas connected synderesis to natural law, identifying the first practical principles, of which synderesis is the habit, with the general principles of natural law. He occasionally replaced the word synderesis by the term 'understanding' (intellectus), the intellectual virtue of grasping the first principles of reason in his Summa Theologiae.

Aquinas understood the directives of synderesis as formal principles, not as concrete moral norms. He conceived of synderesis as habitual knowledge. According to him, conscience is the consideration of a specific case in light of one's moral knowledge.

Moral knowledge therefore comprises the first principles of synderesis, as well as more particular moral directives. Aquinas argued that the binding character of conscience, whether erring or not, means that acting against conscience is always evil. As he would say, a conscience may be certain; but that does not mean that it is correct.

[Taking this as a lead, an incorrect moral judgement, even though made by certainty of conscience, would still be faulty, and ultimately guilty].

-o-o-o-o-o-o-o-

To all members of Catholic families who may have read this, may you be blessed, and may the Catholic Church in Canada always remain faithful to its roots, to Christ, who is *"The Way, the Truth, and the Life"*. (**Jn.14:6**). (See Chap.3 – The **WORD**).

-o-o-o-o-o-o-o-

Happy are we if we exercise justice,
And constantly practise virtue.
O God, remember me,
For the love you bear your people,
Come to me as a saviour,
Let me share the happiness of your chosen,
The joys of your nation,
And take pride in being one of your heirs.

(Ps.106(105) vs.3-5)

-o-o-o-o-o-o-o-

CPSIA information can be obtained
at www.ICGtesting.com
Printed in the USA
LVHW082156310722
724844LV00003B/34

9 780228 842378